Fathers & Sons & Sports

Fathers & Sons & Sports

GREAT WRITING BY
Buzz Bissinger,
John Ed Bradley,
Bill Geist,
Donald Hall,
Mark Kriegel,
Norman Maclean,
and others

Introduction by
MIKE LUPICA

Contents

Introduction

◆

MIKE LUPICA

My dad first took me into the room, welcomed me into the company of sports, when I was six.

He had long since completed all the preliminaries, patiently teaching me the rules of baseball, buying me my first bat and glove, giving me a cut-off five-iron and showing me how to grip it, taking me to the park next door to our house and watching as I finally, and with everything I had, managed to heave a basketball to the rim for the first time.

But it was on the day the Giants played the Colts in 1958—the first sudden-death championship game in NFL history, the one that made pro football a big television attraction in this country—that I joined the conversation.

We lived in upstate New York at the time. There was no American Football League, no DirecTV, no NFL Sunday Ticket, no thought even given to letting people watch any matchup they wanted on Sunday afternoon. For me, there was just one game: The football Giants. And now they had beaten Jim Brown and the Cleveland Browns, and they were going up against Johnny Unitas's Colts for the title. So this Sunday was different.

I wasn't just watching with my dad. All of my uncles were there as well. Just like that, I was in. So many things have changed for me in the life I've been lucky to lead since that day in December 1958, but one thing remains the same: There is no game I am watching that I wouldn't rather be watching with my dad. The best days I've had in sports, either in front of a TV screen or at the ballpark, were shared with my dad and my three sons.

(And just for the record: My nine-year-old daughter? When she occasionally sits with me and asks questions about a game I am watching—usually with her brothers out of the room, usually a baseball game—it is a joy of my life. But this is a book about fathers and sons and sports. I'm just doing my job here!)

The first great day was December 28, 1958, Alan Ameche going into the end zone in overtime, sports breaking my heart for the first time.

I remember that play. I remember a big fumble from Frank Gifford. I remember Unitas's near perfection, never missing a receiver or a throw. The rest of it is a blur. What I know now about the game I have filled in over the years: Raymond Berry's catches, the big catch Jim Mutscheller made, Lenny Moore's running, and the plays that Chuckin' Charlie Conerly made for the Giants. Because it was such an iconic game I have, over time, been able to remember what I had forgotten. ESPN Classic will do that for you.

What I have never forgotten and never will forget is the magic in the room as I sat on the couch next to my father. The excitement of it all. The air in the room.

My friend Seymour Siwoff, who founded the Elias Sports Bureau, once described sports as you talking about a moment and me talking about the same moment and the air in between us.

I remember sitting next to my dad and I remember that air.

There was no formal announcement, no rite of initiation. It was as if my dad took me by the hand and we entered this world together, the world of shared memories and a shared language and all the things, good and bad, that sports make you feel.

The best part of it is, we are still in it. Together. And now my own sons are there with us. I'm sure you have your own home court crowd, the one arena in sports where you most want to be.

That is mine.

My oldest boy is in college now, Boston College, my alma mater. My mom and dad live in New Hampshire, in the house we moved into in 1964. The house is less than an hour from downtown Boston, so this past October I arranged for my pop and my son to attend the first two games of the Red Sox-Indians American League Championship Series.

I was going up to Boston for the series' last two games, so I watched the first two at home. And there was a moment in Game One when the count went to 3-2 on Manny Ramirez and the crowd at Fenway got up, the way it does, and the cameras began to take random shots, the way cameras do.

Suddenly there they were.

My son was up first. My dad, who was eighty-three at the time, took a little longer to get out of his seat, though he would tell me later that it was only because his grandson, the college boy, was blocking his way.

There they were, the two of them front and center on my television screen, side by side. There was my son where I had always been, next to my dad.

We had TiVo on the set I was watching, so I was able to record the moment the way you would record a great play, a great shot or catch or swing of the bat. Because this wasn't a picture worth a thousand words, it was worth a million. Because there it was, the bond between fathers and sons I am trying to explain here as best I can:

That bond being passed on.

This introduction is about my own father-son memories. I'm sure you have your own, about your first bat and glove, about your first trip to the ballpark, Fenway Park or Yankee Stadium or Wrigley or Dodger Stadium. My dear friend Pete Hamill remembers everything—and I mean everything—about the day he went to Ebbets Field with his father, the two of them seeing for the first time Jack Roosevelt Robinson play a game of baseball for the Brooklyn Dodgers.

"That was the day the template was cut," is the way Hamill puts it.

You never need TiVo for a day like that.

Here's another childhood memory from upstate New York. We lived more than five hours away from Yankee Stadium by car, and so there were years when the only big-league baseball I saw was the old exhibition game they used to play in Cooperstown on Hall of Fame weekend. One year, by sheer blessed chance, the Yankees were in that game.

Only once we were inside the little antique ballpark, it began to rain. And it wouldn't stop raining. And before long it was end-of-the-world rain, and everybody was running back to the streets of the little town, looking for some sort of cover, any sort of cover. Including my dad and me.

We managed to find an awning on Cooperstown's main street. As we were catching our breath, soaking wet, we turned around. There, in full uniform, standing next to us in his No. 14, was Bill "Moose" Skowron. The ballplayers, it turned out, had come running to town like everybody else.

My dad is a sweet, shy, gentle man. But now he tapped

Skowron on the shoulder, introduced himself, and said, "Mr. Skowron, I'd like you to meet my son, Michael."

The big man shook my hand.

The first big leaguer I ever met.

Another door in sports opened by my dad.

He never pushed them on me. He has always loved sports, has always been passionate about his teams, but never allowed that passion to run wild. Never allowed sports to lose its wonderful place in his wonderful life. If he has passed on anything to me, it is that.

My friend William Goldman, who wrote *The Princess Bride* and *Marathon Man*, who won Oscars for *Butch Cassidy and the Sundance Kid* and *All The President's Men*, is always talking about how he instantly finds a comfort zone in any Hollywood meeting if somebody in the room is a sports fan.

"I know we've got a common language," Bill says.

I got that language from my dad. It isn't something I remember learning, the way I remember struggling to learn Spanish or French in school. There is no day that I remember my dad sitting me down and telling me he was going to teach me the language of the infield-fly rule. We just started communicating through sports as well as we communicated through anything.

And still do.

When Jack Nicklaus came from behind to win the Masters in 1986, with his son Jackie on the bag that day, I probably called my dad ten times over the last nine holes. It was the year before my first son was born. So when the big things happened in sports, it was still my pop and me.

A year earlier, we had been in his den in New Hampshire when Doug Flutie completed that Hail Mary pass against Miami the day after Thanksgiving, the most famous pass not just in the history of his school and mine, but in all of college football.

Once more, my dad and I were in front of a television, two big kids hugging each other and doing this crazy dance in front of the set, sharing the magic of that moment, breathing in the intoxicating air in the room.

I remember Flutie on the run and the ball in the air and then Flutie sprinting down the field to celebrate with his buddy, Gerard Phelan, the guy who had somehow caught that ball.

I see it now and wish I was there.

Not in the Orange Bowl.

But back in the room with my father.

So I hope you enjoy reading about fathers and sons and sports in the pages of this book. I have my memories. The writers of these pieces have their own.

Ron Reagan writes about the first time he beat his father in the swimming pool, a boy of twelve edging out his sixty-year-old dad. Poet Laureate Donald Hall writes lyrically about the simple act of playing catch with your father, and John Buffalo Mailer writes about the morning his famous father, Norman, led him to believe—at the age of three—that he had the best right-hand cross in the world.

John Ed Bradley explains the lessons he learned about football and life from his father the coach, and the great Henry Aaron dreams of making it big in sports. John Jeremiah Sullivan writes about seeking to understand his own deceased sportswriter father by looking into the man's love of sports, particularly his love for the horse Secretariat.

And pardon my prejudice, but there is a particularly wonderful piece written by my friend Jeremy Schaap about his late father, Dick. Maybe you know this and maybe not, but I was lucky enough to have Dick Schaap as a friend and mentor for more than thirty years of my life, and then lucky enough to sit next to him on ESPN's *The Sports Reporters* for more than a decade.

Besides the one next to my dad and my boys, it is the best seat I've ever had.

In "A Father's Gift," Jeremy writes about how Dick missed two of Reggie Jackson's three home runs in Game Six of the 1977 World Series because he was off getting hot dogs and sodas for his son.

In "Holy Ground," Wright Thompson explains the pain of losing his dad to cancer before he could deliver on a promise to share a golf trip to the Masters Tournament with him.

These are only a few of the fine pieces in this book. I urge you to read them all. In the end, they will do exactly what sports does. They will make you feel and they will make you remember.

I write young adult novels now, have for years. The first was *Travel Team*, a book that really began for me—unexpectedly—the first time sports broke the heart of my second son, when he was cut from a seventh-grade travel team for being too small. I started a basketball team that year for all the boys who got cut, and it became one of the greatest sports experiences, one of the greatest seasons, of my life.

My son will remember that season the way all the boys on that team will remember it. But more than a season he didn't expect to have, one that none of the boys expected to have, it was an adventure my boy and I shared together.

My newest novel, *The Big Field*, is built around the strained relationship between the hero and his father, a failed ballplayer. The two think the bond between them is irretrievably lost until their common love of sports helps them find the love they still have for each other.

Again: I have my own stories, my own memories, about my dad. You have yours. The writers of these stories have theirs. The language, though, the language doesn't change.

Neither does the air in the room.

Mike Lupica
January 2008

Fathers & Sons & Sports

Worlds Apart

◆

TOM FRIEND

There's where your dad used to live, right above the strip club. There's the 7-Eleven where he used to steal doughnuts. Those are the bushes where he used to have sex. That's the street corner where he robbed a stinking drunk. That's the jail where his mom was locked up.

What, you're scared of this place? You don't even know this place. Your dad went to bed hungry here. His only meal of the day was a school lunch (unless they served brussels sprouts).

Having electricity on a Tuesday didn't guarantee he'd have it on a Wednesday. He was evicted twenty-three times. He got a new pair of sneakers once every three years. He got a girl pregnant at fourteen. Your mom.

You guys like your life, right? You've got a computer and an iPod and an Xbox. Your dad didn't even have a mailbox. You live in a 14,000-square-foot mansion. It's not in the 'burbs, it's beyond the 'burbs. It's on a mountain. It's got nine showers for the humans and one for the dog. It's got a pool table and a pool. It's got a theater downstairs and a lighthouse upstairs. It's got a maid's quarters, even though there's no maid, and a wine cellar, even though there's no wine. It's got an arcade room, a steam room, a workout room and rooms to be named later. It's got a Super Bowl ring.

How old are you three kids now—fifteen, twelve and nine? It's time you realize your dad wasn't always a filthy rich football player. He used to be nothing, used to get spit on, shot at, trash-talked.

He used to clean his sneakers with a toothbrush, used to heat his apartment by sticking a lit match in a mayonnaise jar. But you guys? You've got flat-screen TVs in your rooms, two dozen pairs of sneakers in your closets, a gazebo in your backyard. You've gotten kind of soft, kind of complacent, kind of … country club.

So your dad's decided to drive you down your mountain today, decided to take you straight past the hookers and the houses that are boarded up. He's decided to drop you off in the hood, right in front of a ratty Boys & Girls Club. He's just going to drop you and drive off. For your own good.

See you in three hours.

◆ ◆ ◆

It isn't by the book, but, the Dolphins' thirty-year-old safety Tebucky Jones could be NFL Father of the Year for this.

One year ago, he took three well-mannered, well-dressed, well-fed kids and sent them, argyles and all, back to his own cruel childhood. It wasn't entirely necessary and it wasn't entirely safe, but he couldn't rely on *MTV Cribs* to toughen them up. He had to do it himself.

They just weren't taking his cues. They'd see him turning off light switches behind them or spending entire days with his rottweiler, and they wouldn't think to ask why. They didn't know that, growing up in the New Britain, Connecticut, slums, he found a puppy pit bull. That he hid the pit bull in his closet for days, knowing his mother, Maryann, didn't need another mouth to feed. That his mother heard barking in Tebucky's room one day and that Tebucky tried saying, "That's me barking." That it broke his nine-year-old heart to send that puppy back to the streets.

They didn't know that one of his apartments burned to a crisp, that he was homeless in junior high for weeks, that he stole five hundred dollars from a drunk because it was either that or sleep on a sewer cap.

5

They didn't know that he used to cut a hole in his jacket, stroll into a 7-Eleven and stuff candy into the hole. Or that he led a search party for his mother one night, not realizing she'd been thrown in the slammer on drug charges. Or that he'd seek refuge at the New Britain Boys Club, even though there were hookers across the street and gang members outside firing guns.

So he told them everything. He told them about his one pair of sneakers, how he had to wear the same size 8's from fifth to seventh grades even though, by the end, they were four sizes too small for him. How the sneakers were cheap red and black Sprints. How he put a piece of tape over the insignia so they'd look like Air Jordans. How, in school one day, his cousin tore the piece of tape off, and how he could barely face the world after that. He told them that a classmate named Jenny felt compassion for him. That she'd bring him food from Burger King late at night. That Tebucky's mom didn't want Jenny around and that Jenny's middle-class parents didn't want Tebucky around. That Tebucky used to throw pebbles at her bedroom window to get her to sneak out. That they'd go fool around in the bushes.

He told them that when he was fourteen, he got Jenny pregnant. That his family and friends told him to dump her. That they told him to choose football over a ball and chain. That he chose football for a while, until he met his baby girl, four-week-old Letesha. That the minute Letesha threw up all over him, he was hooked. He decided he wasn't giving up anything. Not the football and not the ball and chain.

Jenny told them how rare it was for a teenage dad to stick by his girl and his kid. Or kids. When Tebucky was sixteen, Jenny got pregnant with Tebucky Jr., and when he was nineteen, she got pregnant with Malique. Jenny told them that when she was living at home and he was up at Syracuse playing football, he proposed to her in the middle of a long-distance phone call. That he brought them all up to campus even though he had no money in his wallet. That they had no car and had to take buses in subzero weather. That they were so poor, he stole a Christmas tree for them one December.

The kids didn't recall any of it. What they do remember is draft day 1998, when Bill Belichick and the Patriots made Tebucky a surprise first-round pick. And when their dad's signing bonus arrived in the mail, all $2.65 million of it. And when they moved into their first house, in Wrentham, Mass. And when they saw the neighborhood children arriving at school in BMWs and Jaguars.

What they remember is the Patriots winning the Super Bowl after the 2001 season. And their dad becoming a free agent, and being named the Patriots' franchise player. And him eventually being traded to the Saints, who gave him a new contract worth $29.2 million, including a $6 million signing bonus. They remember Mom and Dad buying an off-season home in Connecticut for $2.96 million. A home just down the street from 50 Cent. A home only ten minutes from the hood where their dad grew up.

They remember the rottweiler their dad bought to make up for the pit bull he couldn't keep. And the 400 pairs of sneakers he bought to make up for his one pair of phony Air Jordans. They remember him cleaning all 400 pairs with a toothbrush. And him buying Christmas trees and turning every holiday into a free-for-all. "I've gotten 'em two Xboxes, Sony PlayStation, Dreamcast," Tebucky says. "Every time something came out, they got it."

But they also remember their dad getting frustrated with them. Letesha would sit quietly in her room and wouldn't play sports. Malique, the youngest, wanted to play hockey, of all things. And young Tebucky, perhaps the best athlete of them all, was getting pushed around in basketball.

It's not that the kid wasn't strong. He was a young Adonis, already 5'9" in the fifth grade. But he was almost too sweet of a kid. He dressed in sweater-vests, was called Prep at school and wanted to play college basketball at Duke. His dad would go to his grammar school basketball games and be horrified. The competition was mediocre, and when the team finally played against an ornery city team from East Hartford, the boy crawled into a shell. The inner-city kids talked trash and young Tebucky bit his lip. He stopped going to the basket. He wasn't fighting for rebounds. He'd overpass. He had morphed into a stereotypical player from the 'burbs.

"He'd call me soft every day," young Tebucky says.

"Not every day," Jenny says. "Stop exaggerating."

"Well, we were getting a little bit soft," Malique says.

To his dad, there was nothing worse. His kids were book smart; he was street smart. His roots were in the slums; their roots were at Abercrombie & Fitch. He asked around the NFL and realized that this is what sometimes happens to the kids of pro athletes. It's not their fault, it's money's fault. Tebucky started getting more impatient with them. He'd tell them to stop lying on the couch, to open the living room shades. He'd call them Pudding Pops, his code for softy. If they wouldn't eat, he'd say, "I'd be 6'6" instead of 6'2" if I'd had the food y'all have." He began making them run suicide sprints in their indoor gym. They'd ask him for cash to go to the mall, and he'd say, "What do I look like, Bank of America?"

"I was getting fed up," Tebucky says. "I wanted them to know how lucky they were, that when I told them stories about my life, it wasn't bull. A lot of kids are snobs and look down on people. But I wanted 'em to know we're all human. I wanted 'em to see both sides of life."

By the spring of 2004, he decided there was only one option. He piled his three kids into his Mercedes and drove them ten minutes down the hill to his old Boys & Girls Club in New Britain. At the curb, he simply opened the car door and said, "Bye." And all the inner-city kids inside saw it. They saw three pampered kids duck out of a Mercedes and walk smack into their world.

Here comes the raw meat.

✦ ✦ ✦

The first day was all about money. The club kids wanted to know how much they had. And how many Mercedes they owned. And how many sneakers. And how big a house. And how much spare change they had in their pockets.

"Can I borrow seventy-five cents?" a young boy asked Malique.

Malique, the most outgoing of the children, said, "What do I look like, Bank of America?"

Before dropping them off, Tebucky had wagged a finger in their faces, telling them, "There are gonna be kids swearing in there and kids begging in there. And if they see you're soft, they're going to take your money. So don't be soft." He'd also told them, "You guys have to stick together.

"You have to have each other's backs. It's the way it works in the hood. Someone messes with one of you, you three better mess with him. Or you have to deal with me."

They heeded every word. After Malique's "Bank of America" comment, young Tebucky and Letesha shadowed their little brother while he played video games. And while he shot hoops. And while he hung out. When their dad picked them up three hours later, they told him nobody messed with them. Good, he said. Because they were going back next week.

The second day was all about clothes. The Boys Club kids wore oversize pants, oversize shirts and undersize undershirts, while Tebucky's kids wore snug-fitting outfits from Gap. Young

Tebucky remembers feeling self-conscious, remembers thinking, "I'm not comfortable. I'm not used to being around people from the projects." There'd been some ridicule that day—the name Prep came up again as he hung out—and when the kids got home that night, they decided there would not be ridicule again.

The third day was all about fitting in. Young Tebucky and Malique had always watched hip-hop videos—"I liked the clothes they wore," young Tebucky says—but were never motivated to wear XXXLs until that week. And when big Tebucky took them to the Boys Club, he couldn't believe his eyes. "Their pants were hanging down and their underwear was showing," he remembers. "They had little earrings, little chains. They walked out of the car like they were Puff Daddy."

The fourth day was all about sports, particularly for young Tebucky. He was the shyest of the three kids, the one his mom was worried sick about. "I thought, oh my god. We're putting them in with ghetto kids and haters," she says. "And I was especially worried for young Tebucky. He talks very proper. Even though he started dressing a little gangsta style, you could tell this boy's from the suburbs; he's not from the hood."

The minute he started playing at the Boys Club, young Tebucky knew it was a different game. Elbows were flying. If someone made a sweet spin move or blocked a shot, the players would ooh and ah. Young Tebucky never saw that in the 'burbs. At the Boys Club, everybody on the court got a nickname. It'd be

Melon Head or Peanut Head or Something Head. Always something with the head.

This is what young Tebucky was learning at the Boys Club: the fine art of talking trash. Big Tebucky says he didn't want to turn any of his kids into "thugs," and he could tell they still knew right from wrong. But he wanted them to speak up, particularly young Tebucky.

By the end of that spring, big Tebucky ended the Boys Club experiment. None of the kids had been bullied and none of them had become the Bank of America. Letesha, the oldest, soon signed up for the school volleyball and softball teams. Malique signed up for Pee Wee football, and began wearing do-rags and sucking all day on lollipops. He was still a smart, polite kid under the getup, but he couldn't help it now: he had to wear black every day.

But young Tebucky remained somewhat of an introvert, so late that same spring, his dad made him try out for New Britain's inner-city AAU team. The team was run by big Tebucky's high school coach, Stan Glowiak, but young Tebucky was convinced he wouldn't make the team. "You think I was gonna cut him and deal with his old man?" Glowiak says. "No way."

They played a doubleheader one morning, and during the first game young Tebucky pulled up lame with a blister on his foot. His new sneakers were the cause, and it looked like he was done for the day. But just when his dad was about to come out of the stands to call his son a Pudding Pop, young Tebucky borrowed Glowiak's kicks—beat-up running shoes—and suited up for the second game. Scored thirty-six points, too. Got hammered into a padded wall and hammered the guy back. Big Tebucky pumped a fist. "If it weren't for the Boys Club, I'd have sat that game out," young Tebucky says. "The Boys Club woke me up."

That August, big Tebucky went back to New Orleans for the season, leaving his family behind in Connecticut. Other than during the bye week, he barely saw them. He threatened to put a surveillance camera in the mansion and watch them via the Internet, but it was all talk. So when the season ended—with him about to go to Miami as a free agent—he had no idea what he was coming home to: sheltered kids or independent kids.

Letesha was fine. Some girls at school had begun calling her "rich bitch," but she didn't back down. The rift was mostly over a boy, and, in the end, she got the boy. And invitations to the mall.

Malique was fine too. He had the confidence, as a fourth-grader, to crash a seventh-grade dance at a community center. And in his do-rag, he won the dance contest.

As for young Tebucky, he was in size twelve sneakers now, same as his dad. As a 5'10" twelve-year-old, he could grab the rim now, same as his dad. He cleaned his sneakers with a toothbrush now, same as his dad. He played pickup ball against twenty-year-olds now, same as his dad.

Right after the season, the two Tebuckys played a game of one-on-one, and big Tebucky realized there'd be no need for the

Boys Club anymore. Not only did young Tebucky foul his father hard on the neck and elbow him hard in the chest, he had a name for the old man:

Bean Head.

It's always something with the head.

Tom Friend has been a senior writer at ESPN the Magazine *since its inception in 1998. He has previously worked for* The New York Times, The Washington Post, *the* Los Angeles Times, *the* National Sports Daily, The Kansas City Star, *and the* San Jose Mercury News. *Friend has also authored two books—*Educating Dexter *and* Jack of All Trades. *His work has been reprinted in* Best American Sports Writing *and he was named one of America's top twenty sportswriters by* Men's Journal. *He is a graduate of the University of Missouri and lives in Southern California with his wife and two children.*

A Father's Small Hope

◆

PAUL SOLOTAROFF

On the patio of the house I've moved out of, my soon-to-be ex-wife dribbles a ball, counting down the time. "Five seconds, four ..." Elaine sets her feet and heaves a shot that bows the plastic rim before rattling off. I rebound her miss off the backboard. Luke, our seven-year-old only child, stares at me, befuddled. He isn't used to seeing me in his mother's yard, almost two years after our separation, and is even less used to seeing us horse around as if those years, and the last few of our eleven-year marriage, hadn't been deadly. But it's the first mild evening of a belated spring, and Elaine and I are gamely making an effort. Not merely to get on better, but to draw him out of the house, where he is more and more the hostage of his disorder.

Sizing a free throw, I glance at Luke, who has begun to point with both hands to the door. We've been out here five minutes, and already the uh-oh moment, his balky signal that he's had it with novelty. What he wants, with a tireless monomania, is the same thing he's wanted for the past four years: to be alone with his TV/VCR. There, he will swap Elmo tapes in and out of the slot while hopping up and down, flapping his arms. Left alone for any time, he'll strip off his clothes, then alternate between flapping his arms and fondling himself. With my stress level spiking—I am always clenched now, conditioned by his history of seizures and meltdowns to anticipate the worst—I hit upon a thought. Tossing a flat shot off the chest-high rim, I grab the ball and hand it to him. Luke stares at it, turning it this way and that, as if trying to recall this Spalding fellow whose name appears between the seams. "Jam it!" says his mother. "Throw it down!" For encouragement, she pelts him with kisses.

He reflects a while longer, looks at both of us, and tosses the ball behind him in the weeds. "Bye," he says, and starts up the stairs, unbuttoning himself as he goes. He stops and waves, my receding son. "Bye," he says. "Buh-bye."

From the beginning the signs were bad, and they worsened as we went forward. Luke was floppy at birth, with muscles so weak his mouth wouldn't latch to his mother's breast. He was late rolling over, later sitting up, and was so late learning to crawl we thought he had cerebral palsy. Those first years were a roundelay of doctors, with each more stumped than the last. Meanwhile, time passed, and Luke's companions stood up on two legs and left him, running after the other kids in the park. Here was a parent's vision of hell: a child whose nameless condition was so dire that two-year-olds had cast him out.

We swept in quickly and found therapists and teachers, getting him home-based treatments early on. Disabled though he was, I was fixed on raising a son who could delight in his body like other kids. Even before he crawled I put him on the floor, rolling balls to him in our master bedroom. He had a natural arm and loved playing catch, though he lacked the least instinct for cupping his hands and seeing the ball safely into his grasp. Still, I took heart and bought him the equipment: a Little Tikes backboard with a weighted base, a football net with a ball he could kick (with help) and a set of oversize bowling pins that he thought were a scream to knock down.

Approaching his third birthday, he suddenly started walking, and our hopes briefly jumped up with him. Soon he was running, and I took him to the park with our trove of balls to try to engage him with boys his age. It worked for a while; he got a kick out of making other kids chase down his errant throws. But one day a boy plucked the ball from his hands, and Luke howled as though he'd been slugged. It was a tantrum from hell, wild-eyed and gasping, the other parents looking on in horror. In a matter of weeks he lost interest in the park, and jerked away when I drove up to it, screaming his one word: "No!" The greater loss, though, was his pleasure in playing ball, which was replaced by the VCR. Before long he'd doubled his working vocabulary, grunting "Elmo" (actually, "Uh-mo") until I caved.

That summer there was another significant development: Luke finally had a proper diagnosis. He has, we learned, a syndrome called Fragile X, a single-gene mutation at the base of the X chromosome that wreaks a range of nervous-system havoc. That flawed gene, identified in 1991 through an outgrowth of the Human Genome Project, fails to make an important protein that regulates other proteins in the brain. No one knows the exact function it serves, but without it key brain cells develop abnormally and their ability to send their signals is impaired. Physical manifestations are, for the most part, innocuous (long faces, prominent ears, and in males, enlarged testes), and kids so afflicted are usually otherwise healthy and can expect to live to old age. But the effect on developing brains is profound, a cure through gene therapy is decades off, and a promising class of experimental drugs is just now entering human trials. For the estimated 90,000 sufferers in America alone, relief is years away.

In its mildest, which is to say rarest, form, Fragile X causes modest retardation and a host of social dysfunctions: shyness, slurred and/or repetitive speech, and obsessive-compulsive behaviors, to name just some. In the middle range, those symptoms are more pronounced and often appended by neuropsychiatric woes: panic, phobias, sleep disorders, and severe overreactions to bright light and loud noises. And then there are the kids in the bottom bracket whose nervous systems are under sensory assault. Picture having to live in a video arcade with the volume and wattage up full, where everyone around you is racing past, speaking Mandarin at the top of their lungs. Your shirt feels like Brillo, your shoes like cement, and the breeze on your skin like the thwack of a soaking towel that's been left to chill in the fridge.

That, in a nutshell, is my little boy, who, like many of his profoundly affected peers, has autism, epilepsy and an IQ we can't measure because he can't, or won't, follow instructions. He is months or possibly years from being toilet-trained, eats with his hands and has no capacity to tie his shoes, though he is Harry Houdini himself at getting out of them.

We have tried (and tried) to ease his symptoms with all the conventional treatments, but have gotten very little bang for our hard-earned bucks in speech, occupational and physical therapies. The only thing that's helped, and that just barely, is a mix of powerful drugs: Luvox for mood swings, Abilify for attention-deficit problems and Trileptal for seizure disorder. Forty years ago most kids like mine were raised in institutions. Luke may still wind up in a residential school, coming home to Elaine or me on weekends. For now, we're doing all we can to fend that off, day by day.

One night, after an hour of ritualized groveling to get Luke to sleep, I collapse on the couch to watch TV. Spinning the dial, I happen upon a profile of a man named Izzy Paskowitz. A goateed, lion-maned surfer who was a longboard champion in the early nineties, Paskowitz runs a bustling surf camp on the beaches of San Diego with his wife Danielle and several of his eight siblings. He and Danielle also founded something called Surfers Healing, a series of traveling one-day surf camps for autistic children. He has a kid so afflicted himself, a boy named Isaiah whose development was normal till he woke at eighteen months "changed totally." His language was gone, he became agitated and began throwing tantrums that were hard to quell.

Paskowitz, whose father was a champion surfer and who had planned on passing the mantle to his son, handled the situation badly for a time. He went out on tour and stayed there for months, living the hang-ten high life of twelve-foot waves and too much to drink. Returning from the road, he found his wife at her wits' end and his young son "lost, a different person." At the beach one day Isaiah was throwing a fit when Izzy had a bold idea. Grabbing his board in one hand and his four-year-old in the other, he jumped in the water and paddled out. Riding his first swell straight into shore, Isaiah grew calm, then exultant. Over days and months of riding point on Izzy's board, a different boy emerged from his cell of symptoms. He began to talk again, his mood improved, and his frustration lessened; clearly there was something tonic about sluicing through water on a shim of fiberglass and foam.

Surfers Healing, born from that eureka moment, has grown into a bona-fide movement. This year, its sixth, it's staging twelve free events in surf towns across America. For some kids it's a one-shot day at the beach; for others, the beginning of a long-term connection to the ocean and its liberating charms.

My first thought, after I blot tears with my sleeve, is to track down Paskowitz's private number and take Luke to San Diego for a week of lessons. But Elaine quite rightly will hear none of it, having flown Luke cross-country before. "It was non-stop hell," she says on the phone. "He slipped out of the seat, screamed, and threw up. It lasted the whole flight back. Either fly the guy here to New York or have him meet you in Florida, but two hours on a plane is Luke's limit."

Alas, it is April, and the Atlantic is the temperature of rigor mortis. As far south as Virginia it is penguin cold, and there are no waves in Miami. I put in some phone calls: I was looking for someone local, an experienced surfer who has worked with special kids and will have the fortitude to handle Luke's freak-outs. He abhors being touched by people he doesn't know and is acutely fearful of new experiences, which is commonplace among autistics. Add to this the fact that Luke is frightened by waves, and whoever comes along will be sorely tested trying to manage this young boy's terror. To say nothing, of course, of mine.

I grew up a kid whose father left and who experienced his leaving as a death. In a household whose climate was for the most part governed by my manic-depressive mother, my father was the mast that my brother and I clung to, an anchor of sanity and poise. It was he who awoke at two in the morning to nurse me through asthma attacks, chatting while the steam in the bathroom did its work. It was, he explained, to the extent that anyone could then, the logic of my mother's moods. We were intensely bonded, he and I, and then suddenly the Christmas I was nine, he was gone, driven across town by her ultimatums and endless grievances. I saw him on Wednesdays and alternate weekends, but for years I was hollow, a walking cipher. Some holes you fill, and some you don't—not, at least, until you're a father yourself.

Like a lot of men lugging around painful pasts, I had big plans for my son. From birth, if not conception, his brain would be steeped in the amniotic fluid of sports and books. He'd grow up that rarity who could hit a curve and describe it afterward in compound clauses. But the boy I sired proved unable to speak his own name. The despair was like a dead weight on my chest. To lift it, I tried the only thing I knew, which was to get him moving again. I brought him to public pools in Brooklyn, where he flapped and thrashed and clung on tight, refusing to learn to swim. I took him sledding, but our first spill freaked him out and he wouldn't get back on the sled. We drove to the country to hike through the woods and visit a working farm; the smell of cow dung made him sick and he tugged at my arm to go. Everywhere I turned, doors were slamming shut, locking us both in a dingy room, the blinds drawn and Elmo on the TV.

It is impossible to convey what this has meant to me psychically. I have the requisite words, but they will ring hollow if you haven't yourself met great sadness. On the worst days I look into Luke's eyes and find them empty as pools. I know there's life inside them, but don't know how I know; there are times when he's just gone and has left no note.

Two days after my talk with Elaine there is a call from a man who wants to take my son surfing. I have my doubts—I have nothing but doubts—but Elliot Zuckerman won't hear them. "Your kid will love this. Guaranteed. Never had a kid who didn't, and I've taught hundreds." Zuckerman, fifty-two, is an ex-pro surfer who grew up riding the chop near New York City. Just past the line where the borough of Queens ends and Long Island's suburbs begin, a sprig of land juts into the Atlantic, forming a sort of bivouac in the sea. Most of the men raised in these sandy flats have been dropping in on waves since they could dress themselves; Zuckerman is the unelected mayor of the beach. He has a frenzied day job as the director of building services for the New York Mercantile Exchange, then comes home at night and spends hours in the water, teaching outlanders from the city how to catch waves. His classes are so popular that a few of the townspeople have come to resent him, so he's tried to limit the size of his groups.

Today, however, this is not a problem; it's just me, Luke, and Zuckerman on the sand. There is a good reason we have the place to ourselves: the water is a blue-black 48°F.

Zuckerman, all chest and cantaloupe shoulders, has already donned his winter wetsuit. Now he has the task of putting my son in one. Luke, as I had dreaded during the drive out here, wants none of it. He kicks, sobs, and arches his back. As we struggle to pull the neoprene past his waist, he pierces me with a look of horror. By the time we get the shin-high boots on his feet and the frog-webbed gloves on his hands, I'm close to tears myself. "All right, Dad, relax," says Zuckerman. "The next time you see him he'll be blissed."

He picks my son up, grabs the foam-core board, and marches into the four o'clock tide. I hear Luke sobbing till they're fifty yards out, after which there's only the cawing of the gulls. The ocean, as luck has it, is small today, a lumpy blanket of threadbare waves, none of them taller than chest high. In order to get closer to where my son is bobbing, I run out onto a jetty. The rocks are abraded to a glassy finish and a couple of times I almost skid right off them. It is tediously slow going, and before I'm out there Luke has caught his ride. Both he and Zuckerman are on their bellies, barrelling toward shore on a fat four-footer. Luke, whose expression is first stricken, then shocked, suddenly drops into a grin so big I see spray go into his mouth. He is chattering something that I'm close enough to hear, but the world, for some reason, has gone mute. It's a good couple of seconds before I figure out why: I am laughing and sobbing at the top of my lungs while hopping on the rocks in bare feet. There are several teens fishing for trout nearby, and they look me over like some six-toed frog that turned up on their hook. "Lukey's surfing!" I yell, still pogo-sticking. "My little boy is surfing!"

I start back to shore, thinking it's over and done with; Luke got his big ride and we can all go home now. This was a lovely idea and we'll definitely return—in August, when it's, you know, summer. But as he and Zuckerman reach the shallows Luke rolls off and stands up. "More!" he orders, pointing to sea, and to my utter disbelief, out they paddle. For almost an hour they chase waves, catching several good ones all the way in. My heart is in my throat the entire time; this man, a complete stranger, has my child in his arms and has worked some ocean voodoo on his mood. Luke's lips turn blue, then his nose and brow, but damn it all, he's not leaving. Finally, we get him out and peel the wetsuit off him. A huge, dazed smile spreads across his face. "Yay!" he crows, applauding himself. "All riiight!" he keeps repeating as I dry him.

That night we go back to Zuckerman's house and set Luke up in the media room. I'm emotionally spent, and when Zuckerman's wife Stephanie asks me how it went, I find myself, for perhaps the first time ever, speechless. Luke is anything but; he runs to the TV screen, naming all the objects that he sees: tree, dog, kite, shade. Suddenly, we can't shut this kid up. He isn't just cheerful or glad to be on land; he's positively thrilled with himself. Snuggling in beside me on the leather sofa, he offers me the back of his head to nuzzle, cackling as I oblige. It is unseemly to kiss your child on another man's couch, and embarrassed, I tender apologies.

"Please," says Zuckerman. "Look how happy he is. I've seen it over and over: surfing magic."

Though the notion of surfing as therapy for autism is so novel that no one has studied it, a number of eminent neuroscientists I talk with later are willing to venture a guess as to why it might work. "We know that motor-skill learning has a broad-ranging impact on the nervous system," says William Greenough, an expert on brain development at the Beckman Institute at the University of Illinois, where studies of Fragile X are conducted. "There's increased blood flow to crucial neurons, and the reshaping of abnormal structures in the front brain. But beyond that, surfing may be a vehicle to an emotional breakthrough, a way of reaching under the mask and perhaps connecting to kids like these." Peter Vanderklish, a neurobiologist at the Scripps Research Institute in La Jolla, California, who works on the synaptic mechanisms of learning, offers a slightly more personal take. "I've been surfing for close to thirty years, and my sense is that the sky-and-sea beauty of the sport turns the focus of these kids inside out. They're pulled out of themselves by having to live in the moment, and all their anxieties are pushed aside," he says.

Since the day five years ago when Zuckerman got a call from the mother of a child with autism, he has surfed, free of charge, with dozens of children who run the clinical gamut. Blind kids, deaf kids, quadriplegics—he has put them in the water, with grand results. "It's the same thing each time," he says. "They panic at first, then get totally amped on the wave."

Zuckerman, who is friends with Paskowitz, drops everything in early September to host the Long Beach leg of Surfers Healing. He places himself, his surfboards and a dozen or so instructors at the disposal of the daylong event: "It's like nothing you've ever seen before—between the crowds and media, plus the sixty or eighty families with their kids. They can't stop laughing, or hugging you till it hurts," he says. "It's by far the best day of my year."

He asks us to stay for dinner, but Luke is fading and I need to get him home for his evening meds. Walking to the car, I keep babbling thanks, saying it's been a day I'll never forget. "Oh, and I meant to ask you, what was Luke saying when you guys caught that first wave in?"

Zuckerman laughs, his big shoulders rolling. "Well, he was fussing and fighting the whole way out. But when that big wave came and I threw him on the board, he was yelling 'Whee, whee, whee!' all the way in."

For the next couple of days I scarcely know my child. We go to the park and play for an hour, or what he usually spends there in a month. He makes eye contact longer, seems calmer in his skin, and best of all, initiates the roughhouse games that end in hugs and kisses. I call up Zuckerman and book a second session, and one for me. If my son can brave the water in the middle of April, then his dad can cowboy up and wade in, too.

Here, just maybe, is the thing I've pined for: a chance to engage my child at play and develop something that we can do together. I've no experience with balance sports, unless you count the times I tried to downhill ski, tumbling like a drunk in a whisky barrel going over Niagara Falls. And what begins as a charitably warm mid-spring day turns blustery and damp when we reach the beach; no sooner are we in the water than it starts to pour. "Ignore it," shouts Zuckerman over the wind-whipped waves. "Just do what I tell you and you'll have the time of your life."

He pushes me out to where the sets are forming and turns me around toward shore. "Remember," he says, "come up in one motion! Just pop to your feet and spread 'em!" And with that I'm away, skimming a wash of white foam at what feels like warp speed. My brain yells, "Stand!" and I gamely try to, but my feet yell, "Go to hell!" With Samsonesque effort I get to my knees, and suddenly find myself five feet under, sifting the ocean floor for pretty stones. There is plenty of time to do this, because as soon as one wave lets me up, another right behind it knocks me down.

Zuckerman is unmoved. "I just told you, no knees," he rails. "You wanna start praying, go to church." He sets me up with a baby wave, letting several curlers pass us by. Again I get about halfway up when the board and I part company for creative reasons. Over the next hour and change I fall in every conceivable way, including several rarely seen by orthopedists. Zuckerman shakes his head and barks tough-love encouragement, and as I once more succumb to the laws of gravity and their sadistic pranks on new surfers, I imagine him muttering to himself: "Now which one's disabled again? The son?"

Still, when I clamber out, wring the ocean from my lungs, and collapse on the rain-dark sand, I can't stop grinning. I've never had such fun being an abysmal failure, and want nothing more than to rest a minute, then go back in the water and take my beating. "Is this what you mean by surf magic?" I ask.

"Well, usually you have to surf to feel the magic," Zuckerman says, "but yeah, it's something like that."

I had always assumed that when I connected with Luke on a sport we both enjoyed, it would be on my turf—a game at which I had some middling skill. But as I drive us out to the beach on Pacific Boulevard the following Friday, it occurs to me that just the reverse has happened and I've been dragged, bumbling and stumbling, into his world.

On a surfboard Luke is instantly in his glory, whereas I'm even money for a cracked femur. Perhaps that accounts for my high anxiety as I pull up at the gate. It's one thing to eat it with no one watching, quite another with your boy there. I can only hope he finds my falls funny and doesn't mistake them for seizures.

First Zuckerman, then one of his young assistants, meets us at the beach. The conditions are ripe for our first joint day: small waves, high clouds, and a light puff of breeze that tacks in gently from the south. Today, the Solotaroffs will shred! But Luke throws a fit when he sees the wetsuit, and it takes three of us to get him zipped up tight. It seems grossly unfair to freak him out before he sets foot in the water, but the world is unfair and Elmo can't fix that.

We catch a number of waves, miss a number more, and spend a lot of time in each other's way. At one point I fall, pop my head through the sea foam and see Luke and Zuckerman knifing straight for me. I escape beheading and even get vertical twice, while my son, for all his pique at being shrink-wrapped in rubber, stays in the water for an hour. By the end he and Elliot are a well-oiled unit, going out and coming back in high rotation, wearing loopy grins as they get up. On the drive home to Brooklyn, Luke is silent, staring out of the window in blank exhaustion. So too through dinner of Chinese takeaway, a meal he usually gobbles two-fisted. But in the bathtub he rallies, "reading" *Chicka Chicka Boom Boom*, a book he's known by memory since babyhood.

I towel my child dry, that great, painstaking pleasure, pausing to drink his little-boy scent and kiss the down on his neck. He wheels and surprises me with a hug, an act he confirms by yelling, "Hug!" I hold him so tight it makes my own head reel. Soundlessly we turn an arabesque, a father and young son dancing stag. Carrying him off to bed then, a thought occurs, and I lower him in my arms till he's horizontal. "Lukey's surfing," I sing as we sluice the room. "My brave little boy is surfing."

He puts his arms out to skim the waves and says, "Whee, whee, whee," all the way in.

Paul Solotaroff has been a journalist for eighteen years, having written for Vanity Fair, Esquire, GQ, Vogue, *and* The New York Times Magazine, *among many others. He's currently a contributing editor at* Rolling Stone *and* Men's Journal *magazines, and will publish his third book, a memoir called* The Body Shop, *in 2008. He has been a finalist for both the Pulitzer and the National Magazine Award and his work has been anthologized in* The Best American Sportswriting of the Century.

Little League Confidential

◆

BILL GEIST

It begins early. At Little League games, some fathers have admitted—or mothers have happily testified as hostile witnesses against them—that among the first thoughts they had after learning they were fathers-to-be was a vision of playing catch with their sons in the backyard. And, yes, all right, if need be, with their daughters.

"Honey, did that sonogram indicate if the kid is a lefty or a righty? I was in the sporting goods store today . . ."

The mother of a particularly talented Little League short-stop—a boy I grew to despise as he robotically and errorlessly vacuumed up my son's ground balls and threw him out at first—told me that her husband used to put a portable radio tuned to Mets games up to her stomach when she was pregnant to imprint an interest in baseball on the yet unborn. It seemed a calculated risk. I mean, the kid could be walking around saying "Less Filling! Tastes Great!" the rest of his life, too.

"He was kidding," she said, "I think. He did it a lot."

I told her that was really silly, that I'd waited until the moment of birth, bringing a Rawlings catcher's mitt to the delivery room for use by the obstetrician. Curiously, however, the baby turned out to be a first baseman. Go figure.

Of one thing most expectant fathers are certain: their kid is going to get a much earlier start on the game than they did, a leg up, a competitive advantage. We fathers were never as good at the game as we wanted to be—let alone as good as we told our children we were.

Expectant fathers worry that their offspring will inherit their mediocre hand-eye coordination, their short legs, their clumsy feet. What if my son hates baseball and joins the Audio-Visual Club? What if: My son is a girl? It can happen. It happened to me once.

The first indication of athletic prowess seized upon by fathers is the newborn's APGAR score, a score from one to ten given immediately after the birth to indicate the child's overall health. If the score is a nine or a ten, fathers immediately start thinking: professional triple-A ball or higher; something in the six or seven range might mean the best kid can do is make the high school team. Any score lower than that, and fathers' thoughts naturally turn to adoption.

If the father protests the APGAR score, suing the hospital to upgrade it, he has the makings of a Little League coach!

I bought Willie one of those little baseball uniforms for newborns, the pinstriped ones with the little caps. He looked just like a little Yankee or perhaps a Cub, except for the large patch of drool on his chest.

"Did you see that?!" my wife would shriek, indicating I should punish my son for hitting his grandmother with a stick.

"Yes, I did," I'd answer. "He showed good hand-eye coordination that time, but I truly believe he'd develop more power through the hitting zone if he'd step toward her and extend those arms."

And when she called the office to tell me the baby had just chucked a piece of Waterford across the dining room,

I'd say: "All the way across? Was it on an arc or more of a clothesline throw? How about the accuracy?" She'd hang up.

When he could sit up a little bit, at least when propped, we played a little "catch." It was sort of like one of those carnival midway games: I'd toss a tiny little ball and see if it would come to rest on a roll of fat or a protrusion of some kind, somewhere on his person. When it did, I'd haul out the camcorder.

I figured when the kid could stand, he was ready for batting practice. I bought the Biiiiig, fat, red plastic bat at K-Mart and the really Biiiiig white plastic ball, to get Willie in the swing of things. The technique I recommend is getting on your knees about three feet away (just far enough to not get hit by the Biiiiig bat), yell "Swing!" then toss the ball where the bat might be. (You determine this by having the child take several practice swings.) If the child hits the ball or even swings the bat, you cheer wildly. But don't worry, you will, you will. However, there are other fathers who eschew positive reinforcement, preferring to touch the kid lightly with a cattle prod when he misses. Your call.

Another daydream I had when my wife was pregnant was taking my son to a major league game. Here, fathers also tend to jump the gun a bit. Last year a Bostonian in the stands at the Red Sox spring training camp in Florida held his—snoozing—six-month-old son and said to me: "I just had to bring him down so he could see this."

In my daydream, my unborn son would be sitting there in a blue baseball cap slightly askew or pulled down too far on his head, his little legs dangling, not long enough to reach the ground. He is wearing his little baseball glove on one hand and eating a hot dog with the other, chewing on the ends of both glove and dog. The weather is perfect, of course, sunny and mild, about seventy-six degrees. Our seats are very good. The home team is winning. My son adores me. My tie is loosened, my sleeves are rolled up, and I am (somehow) handsome.

Unfortunately, we lived on the North Side of Chicago when my son was a toddler, so the first game he saw was a Cubs game at Wrigley Field. I know of no finer place to watch a baseball game, although many of us have come to realize that raising a child to be a Cubs fan is a particularly heinous form of child abuse—with lifelong consequences.

Back in Illinois in 1955, my grandfather told me that, well, sure, it had been ten long years since the Cubs had won a pennant but that—doggone it!—I should show some loyalty and stick with 'em! (We lived equidistant between Chicago and St. Louis and I was entertaining the idea of a switch to the Cardinals.) My grandfather was lucky. He died that year. Thirty-seven years later, I'm still waiting for the Cubs to do something.

The reality of taking my son to a ballgame was somewhat less idyllic than the daydream. The home team, as is its custom, was not winning.

And this being Chicago, and the month May, the weather was not quite perfect. It wasn't bad for Chicago, I mean the airport wasn't closed, yet, but it was drizzling a bit, the temperature just warm enough to keep the rain from solidifying. Hell, this was a nice day, springtime in Chicago—time to haul out the lawn furniture.

Willie loved the food. He consumed one hot dog, one bag of peanuts, one box of popcorn, one coke and one ice cream bar in the first five innings. It was not the last we'd see of it.

He asked for, and received, a Cubs cap, pennant and T-shirt. Counting my three beers and hot dog, the afternoon cost just under the Blue Book value of our Datsun wagon.

Midway through the game, the light drizzle turned to rain. But! The Cubs were playing the Padres, and the San Diego chicken saved the day for Willie by running and sliding headfirst across the tarpaulin. By the time the rain delay was over, Willie was asleep. He awakened after the last pitch of the game, and asked: "Did the Cubs win, Dad?"

"Uh, why, yes, son. Yes they did," I answered. Falsely.

Some fathers want to take their kids to ballgames because it reminds them so much of what they did with their own fathers. Not me. I don't think I ever went to a baseball game with my father. We lived in a small town; to go to a baseball game you had to go all the way to Chicago, and no one in his right mind went to Chicago, a city filled with unspeakable traffic and hoodlums—not to mention Democrats! I don't want to say we were provincial, but our high school foreign exchange student was from . . . America. Hawaii.

I have fond memories of lying on the top bunk of the bed I shared with my brother, David, listening to Cardinals baseball games (and Cubs away games) on the radio in the dark while he gently bounced me off the ceiling. Harry Carey, Joe Garagiola and Jack Buck did the Cardinals' broadcasts. There is something wonderful about listening to a baseball game on the radio in the dark.

My brothers-in-law have similar memories of listening to ballgames on summer evenings on the porch in Indianapolis with their grandfather, who was always smoking a cigar. For the moment to be absolutely perfect, the game had to be an obscure one: maybe the Indians and the Orioles.

I met a man in Chicago who loved listening to night games on the radio. He was a lifelong Tigers fan, who had been (tragically) transferred to Chicago at about age fifty. He'd put on his pajamas and drive to the western shore of Lake Michigan, where if he got his car lined up at just the right angle he could pick up Ernie Harwell's broadcasts from Tiger Stadium.

I tried doing that with Willie some, on our screened-in porch in Chicago, and he liked it all right, I guess, but after a while he would always say: "The game's on TV, Daddy."

I know, son, I know.

Bill Geist is the best-selling author of seven books including Fore! Play, The Big Five Oh: Facing, Fearing and Fighting 50, Monster Trucks and Hair In A Can—Who Says America Doesn't Make Anything Anymore?, Little League Confidential, *and* City Slickers. *He has contributed stories to numerous magazines ranging from* Rolling Stone *to* Forbes *to* Esquire. *Geist received two Emmy Awards for his work as a correspondent for* CBS News Sunday Morning. *Prior to joining CBS News, he was a columnist for* The New York Times.

Senior Year

--- ◆ ---

DAN SHAUGHNESSY

*I*t was getting dark and I was standing in the parking lot beyond the rightfield fence at the high school baseball field. The kids call it "third lot." It once provided parking for Newton North High School students, but that was before too many kids got cars, so now it's reserved during school hours for faculty and seniors. At this moment, third lot was two-thirds empty, and the only remaining cars belonged to the players on the baseball team, plus a handful of parents and friends.

I had my keys in my hand. I'd already said good-bye to my old high school coach, who'd made the drive down from New Hampshire to sit with me and watch my son play. It was a cold New England May day and the game was running long and I had to get going. I was due at a wake for the 21-year-old son of my cousin. The wake was taking place in the small town where I was born, an hour's drive to the west, and the notice in the newspaper said visiting hours would be over at 7 p.m.

It had been an emotional day, sitting on the cold metal slats, watching Sam hit, catching up with my old coach, and thinking about what my cousin Mickey was going through. I hadn't seen Mickey in over a year. We were never especially close. That happens when you have fifty-one first cousins and move away after college. But it was easy to remember everything I admired about Mickey. He was a terrific high school athlete, only two years older than I. He seemed to be better than everyone else at everything. Football. Basketball. Skiing. He was strong, tough, skilled, and movie-star handsome. He had his own rock 'n roll band. Chicks dug him and guys wanted to be him. It would have been easy to hate the guy, but he was generous and caring, and when I would see him years later he was always humble about his high school greatness. He'd made a fine life for himself, working for the gas company and raising two kids with his wife. Now he was getting ready to bury his son, young Michael, who had died at home in bed, another victim of the national scourge of Oxycontin. Michael had been a high school football stud, just like his father. He had been good enough to win a scholarship to Wagner College, and there had been a picture in the local newspaper of Michael signing his letter of intent. Now, just a couple of years later, his picture was in the paper again, accompanied by one of those impossibly sad stories about a promising life that ended too soon.

So I was feeling a little guilty as I stood in third lot, jangling my keys and watching the high school baseball game groan into extra innings. I didn't want to miss the wake, but I remembered that earlier in the day Mickey's brother had told me, "We'll be there long after seven." Besides, Sam was scheduled to lead off the bottom of the tenth, and he was due. He had been hitting the ball hard all day, but he was sitting on an 0-4 and I knew his small world would tumble into chaos and panic if he went hitless for the day. Such is the fragility and self-absorption of the high school mind.

I was wondering about my own mind too. I am a professional sportswriter, specializing in baseball. I've been a columnist for *The Boston Globe* for more than 15 years, covering Olympics, Super Bowls, World Series, Stanley Cup Finals, NBA Championships, and Ryder Cups. I traveled with the Baltimore Orioles, Boston Celtics, and Red Sox back in the days when writers really traveled and lived with the ballplayers. I've written 10 books, seven on baseball. I can go to any game, anytime I want. And yet I find myself fixated on the successes and failures of Newton North High School and Sam Shaughnessy, my only son and the youngest of three ballplaying children. Sam's sisters had fun and fulfilling seasons in high school volleyball, field hockey, and softball, and I was amazed at how following their games connected me to their school and our community while kindling so many thoughts of my own high school days thirty years earlier. Probably that's why I found myself suddenly skipping Red Sox road trips and canceling TV appearances because of weather-forced changes in the high school baseball season. Random Sox fans wanted to ask me about Curt Schilling and Jonathan Papelbon. I'd rather talk about Newton North lefthander J.T. Ross.

The score was still tied when Sam walked to the plate to open up the bottom of the tenth, and we were definitely losing the light, making it even tougher to hit. The Braintree coach went out to talk to his pitcher. I looked at the sky. I looked at my watch. This was it. I'd stare through the chain link for one more at-bat, then get in the car. Darkness was going to make this the last inning, even if the score was still tied after ten.

And then, in an instant, the baseball was screeching over the first baseman's head, over the rightfielder's head, over the chain link, and onto the trunk of the 1998 Toyota Corolla that Sam had driven to school that day. It rolled across the lot and came to rest under a tree. I retrieved the ball while he circled the bases.

There was no such thing as a "walk-off" home run when I went to high school. We had read the stories about Bobby Thomson's Shot Heard Round the World, and all my friends and I knew that Pirates second baseman Bill Mazeroski had won the 1960 World Series with a homer in the bottom of the ninth ... but nobody talked about walk-offs until Kirk Gibson dropped one on Dennis Eckersley in the 1988 World Series. Eck popularized the term, and now there are walk-off homers, walk-off doubles, walk-off walks, even an occasional walk-off balk.

In any event, Sam Shaughnessy had his first high school walk-off homer (a drive-off walk-off, given the dent in the Toyota) and knew enough to take his helmet off after rounding third base. He had seen Red Sox slugger David Ortiz do this a lot. A helmetless head is less likely to be pounded by your teammates.

I walked in from rightfield and delivered the baseball to my smiling son. I told him not to worry about the dent on the roof of the trunk (not sure my dad would have been so casual about the damage done). Then I got in my car and drove to the wake.

The country roads took me back. They took me to the place where I grew up, the place where I experienced all the highs and lows that were now happening to Sam. I remembered how it felt to have a moment like he had today and I knew he would hold it in his heart for the rest of his life. Sports have a way of defining our lives, particularly teenage lives. The local high school basketball games were a big deal in my hometown when I was growing up. Most of our parents came to the games and sat in the back row of the small gym. The successes and failures of our team made for conversation around the post office and drugstore in the center of town. We connected through sports.

Two decades later, when my classmates filled out a reunion form, there was a question regarding your favorite high school memory. I was struck by how many answered "Dances after the Friday night basketball games." These were not just the ballplayers and cheerleaders. These were kids who had never played on the team, but as grown-ups they had fond memories of cold nights in a warm gym, when a sporting event was the center of our tiny universe.

The trick is to keep moving forward and not let the glory days of high school become the highlight of your life.

When I wheeled into the funeral home a few minutes after seven, there was a line the length of a football field waiting to pay respects to Michael. Inside, I joined my sisters, cousins, aunts, and uncles and waited for the line to dwindle. In my mind, I pledged not to speak of why I was late or of how the game had ended.

A couple of hours later, the line completely exhausted, I knelt before young Michael and said a prayer. Inside the open casket, there was a photo of Michael celebrating a high school football victory with his teammates. When I stood up, cousin Mickey was there, sobbing, spent, but still strong enough to hug me with the force of a linebacker. It is a universal truth that it's virtually impossible to say anything appropriate in a moment like this. Nothing is worse than a parent losing a child. The loss is unspeakable and incomprehensible. Only those who have experienced such a tragedy can possibly know what it feels like. But the events of my day had given me special perspective, and for once I felt like I knew exactly what to say.

"Michael must have given you a lot of joy."

"Oh, Danny," he said, smiling through the tears, pointing to the photo inside the casket. "You should have seen him play. And not just because he was my son, either. That was the Acton-Boxboro game. One of the greatest nights for all of them. I loved watching him play more than anything."

There it was. I knew then I had made the right decision, staying an extra inning to see the end of a high school baseball game while my sisters and cousins and aunts and uncles were already at the wake. And as I drove home, back across the roads of my youth, I knew I had to write something down.

Dan Shaughnessy is a sports columnist for The Boston Globe. *He has written 11 books, including* The Curse of the Bambino *and* Senior Year, *from which this essay was taken. He has been covering Major League Baseball for more than 30 years.*

It Never Rains in Tiger Stadium

◆

JOHN ED BRADLEY

You should've seen my father's arms. He didn't lift weights or do pushups or exercise them in any way, and yet they were packed tight with muscle. When I was a boy and he lifted his highball in the evening for a sip, a round knot the size of a softball came up under the skin and slowly flattened out when he lowered the glass back down. I loved his arms so much that I memorized every vein, sinew, and golden hair. I knew the wrinkles of his elbows.

In the summer, when he worked for the city's recreation department, supervising the baseball program at the park, Daddy liked to come home for lunch and a nap. He had lemonade and a BLT, then he had me lie close to him on the sofa and he draped an arm around me. "One . . . two . . . three . . . ," he'd count in a whisper, and then he was out, sleeping that easily.

I lay there wondering if I'd ever have arms like his. I needed both hands to travel the distance around his wrist, the tips of my thumbs and fingers barely touching. I felt the hardness of his forearm. I saw how his wedding band fit him like a strand of barbed wire on a tree whose bark had grown around it. He smelled of the grass and the sun, of green and gold days that started early and ended late.

"Were you a good player?" I asked him once, as he was coming awake.

"Was I what?"

"A good player?"

"You want to know if I was a good player?"

"Yes, sir."

"What kind of question is that?"

"I don't know. Did they run your name in the paper a lot?"

He looked at me in a way that let me know he wanted my attention. "None of it matters, John Ed. Was I a good teammate? Did I do my best and give everything I had to help the team? These are the questions you need to be asking."

I wondered how to answer them, these questions he found

of such importance. Many years would have to pass before I was old enough to join a team. He pulled me close again, as if he'd just remembered something. "John Ed?"

"Yes sir."

"Always be humble."

The rest of the year he worked as a civics teacher and coach at the high school in town. The town was Opelousas, on the road between Alexandria and Lafayette, and it was just small enough, at about twenty thousand, to be excluded from Louisiana state maps when TV weathermen gave their forecasts in the evening. In the morning, my father left home wearing coach's slacks with sharp creases and a polo shirt with a Tiger emblem and the words *OHS Football* printed in Halloween orange on the left breast, the lettering melted from too much time in the dryer. A whistle hung from a nylon cord around his neck. It was still hanging there when he returned at night and sat down to a cold supper—the same meal Mama had served her children hours earlier. "You don't want me to warm it for you, Johnny?"

"No, baby. That's okay."

Sometimes in the afternoon, Mama drove me out to the school. She parked under the oak tree by the gymnasium, pointed to where she wanted me to go, and I walked out past a gate in a hurricane fence to the field where my father and the other coaches were holding practice. Four years old, I wore the same crew cut that my father wore. I stumbled through tall grass and out past the red clay track that encircled the field. At home, my father didn't raise his voice, but here he seemed to shout with every breath. A team manager took me by the hand and led me to a long pine bench on the sideline. I sat among Igloo coolers, spare shoulder pads and toolboxes crammed with First Aid supplies. I waited until the last drill had ended and the players came one after another to the coolers for water the same temperature as the day, drunk in single gulps from paper cups shaped like cones. The players took turns giving the top of my head a mussing. "You gonna play football when you grow up?"

"I don't know."

"You gonna be a coach like your daddy?"

"I want to."

Already I was certain that no one mattered more than a coach. I would trade any day to come for a chance to be that boy again, understanding for the first time who his father was. Give me August and two-a-days and a group of teenagers who are now old men, their uniforms stained green from the grass and black with Louisiana loam. Give me my father's voice as he shouts to them, pushing them harder than they believe they can go, willing them to be better. Give me my father when practice is over and he walks to where I'm sitting and reaches his arms out to hold me.

◆ ◆ ◆

I was doomed from the start. If not an LSU football player, what else might I have become? Daddy was so devoted to the team that in the fall he would weigh the merits of each week based on whether the Tigers won or lost on Saturday night. He could be as thoughtful and philosophical as any other high school coach when his own team lost, but he was so devoted to LSU that he was far less understanding when the Tigers from Baton Rouge did. How many times did he leave the house late in a televised game, unable to watch another play? If it looked like the Tigers were going to lose a close one, he was especially long in returning. "Where have you been?" we'd yell at him, when he finally came back inside.

"Nowhere," he'd say. "What happened?"

In those days, LSU games rarely appeared on television more than a couple of times a year. And so we were dedicated listeners to the radio broadcasts and play-by-play announcer John Ferguson. We listened while my mother made potato salad in the kitchen and Daddy barbecued outside on the patio. He'd sit there in a lawn chair, lost in concentration as his chicken burned, a purple-and-gold cap tipped back on his head. His arms, legs, and neck glistened with mosquito repellant, and he sipped from a can of beer wrapped in a foam hugger advertising a local insurance agency. Not far away from his smoldering pit, on a narrow piece of finely manicured St. Augustine, I acted the game out with neighborhood friends, some of us dressed in Little Tiger uniforms. We played until somebody ran into a ligustrum hedge or got clotheslined by a real clothesline, and my father called for an end to the rough-and-tumble and sat me down next to him.

"Settle down now," he'd say. "LSU's on."

In his mind, the football team represented the entire state of Louisiana, and the way the team performed gave the rest of the nation a snapshot of what kind of people we were. Notre Dame's boys might be bigger and stronger than ours, but we weren't afraid to line up against them and see who wanted it more. USC might have better talent—okay, he'd concede that—but you needed more than talent to beat LSU. The Tigers often were underdogs, just like the state of Louisiana. Our players scrapped and hustled and always showed good sportsmanship, never more so than when they lost. On defense, they fought off larger opponents, swarmed to the ball, and made spirited gang tackles, and on offense, everyone gave a second effort, including the quarterback, who wasn't afraid to lower his shoulder and block a player twice his size if that was what it took to win.

Daddy had no use for showboats and loudmouths. He believed that humility was equivalent to class in a man, and nothing pleased him more than to hear a player deflect the praise he'd earned and credit his teammates instead. Players who danced in the end zone after scoring were buffoons. Those who calmly handed the ball to an official were to be admired.

Opelousas produced few athletes who went on to play in Baton Rouge. Those who did carried a large part of my father's identity with them. I remember when John Weinstein and Skip Cormier played on LSU's defensive line in the early 1970s. Both made big hits in important TV games that we watched as a family. Every time the announcers mentioned either Weinstein's or

Cormier's name, Daddy turned in his seat and faced his children. "He's from here," he said.

When Jeff Sandoz, a football and track star at Opelousas High, signed a scholarship with LSU, my father drove me to his house one day after school and parked by the curb in front. We sat there a minute looking at the place, even though we'd seen it a thousand times before. I didn't have to ask him why we had stopped there. When we returned home, he had me go inside and get a football. We spent the rest of the afternoon throwing passes in the yard.

There were great Americans who came from Opelousas, but in my father's mind, none were greater than the town's football players. Alamo hero Jim Bowie, for instance, spent a large part of his childhood in Opelousas. He invented a knife that was good for gutting wild game, but remembering him would've been easier had he played on Saturday in Baton Rouge. Rod Milburn, the track star who won a gold medal in the 110-meter hurdles at the 1972 Munich Olympics, grew up in Opelousas and returned home for a parade in his honor. Daddy enjoyed watching Milburn run, but I'm sure he'd have liked him even more had Milburn used his speed to haul in long passes from quarterbacks in yellow helmets. Paul Prudhomme, the Cajun chef, was another Opelousas boy. In the 1980s, Prudhomme's signature creation, blackened redfish, became so popular that the redfish population in the Gulf of Mexico was threatened with annihilation, prompting the state of Louisiana to impose limits on harvesting it. Prudhomme was a student at Opelousas High when my father was coaching there. One day I asked Daddy what he remembered about the man, and he said, "Well, he wasn't a cook then. And he wasn't a man. Everybody called him Gene."

"That's what you remember? That he wasn't a cook or a man and his name was Gene?"

He shrugged. "What do you want me to tell you?"

"What kind of person was he? What was he like?"

"Like any teenager. I don't know—he was a young kid."

"So he was Gene, a young kid who wasn't a cook or a man yet. That's what you remember?"

"Don't get smart with me, boy."

There was another Prudhomme from Opelousas who went on and made everybody proud. He was Paul's cousin, Remi Prudhomme. At LSU in the early 1960s, Remi earned three letters as an offensive guard. He later played with the Kansas City Chiefs and the Buffalo Bills. In 1970, when the Chiefs faced the Minnesota Vikings in Super Bowl IV, my father pointed out Prudhomme with a finger as he lined up to cover on a kick. I kept one of my own fingers on Prudhomme as he ran down the field trying to make a hit on the return man. When I removed my finger, there was a thin trail in the dust moving west to east, perfectly bisecting the TV screen.

The next time the Chiefs kicked off, we watched as the Vikings' returner fumbled the ball and Prudhomme fell on it. I gave a shout and danced around the room, but my father showed no emotion. The recovery had set up good field position for the Chiefs, who later would score. "He's from here," I said.

"Yes, he is," Daddy answered, failing to register that I was being smart with him.

"Went to the high school."

He got it finally and flicked a finger against the top of my skull.

A year or two later I rode with him one Saturday afternoon to pick up something at Jimmy's Cash Store on the Old Sunset Road. You crossed some railroad tracks and the little package store was there on your left, directly across the blacktop from where Mr. Alfred Lagrange had his yam kiln. Parked out on the white shell lot in front of Jimmy's was a shiny new car growing less shiny by the minute. Every time a vehicle passed down the road dust rolled up and tumbled over in a cloud. It was fine for my father's truck to get dirty—it was a 1963 GMC with rust holes in the bed and dents in the hood—but it was hard to watch it happen to something as pretty as that car.

I waited outside. The store had plate glass windows plastered with white butcher's paper advertising sale items in black and red ink: pork chops, boudin, hogshead cheese, a four-roll package of toilet paper, a box of 12-gauge shotgun shells. Tired of waiting, I let myself out of the truck and went in. I could hear my father's voice coming from the rear of the store, back near the beer cooler. I found him talking to a huge, muscle-bound man wearing a black shirt and blue slacks. "John Ed, come over here, I want you to meet somebody."

It was Remi Prudhomme. He had dark, curly hair kept in place with Brylcreem or some other such product and his face was burned by the sun and showing black stubble that tracked downward to the bottom of his neck and upward to within an inch of his eyeballs. Daddy told me to step closer and have a look at his Super Bowl ring. Remi Prudhomme held his hand out. "You want to try it on? Here. See how it fits."

It was a gaudy thing that sparkled and flashed when you moved it against the ceiling lights. He pulled it off and handed it to me. I could've slipped two fingers into the ring. "You gonna play football when you get older?"

"Yes, sir."

"Who you gonna play for?"

"LSU Tigers."

And then he did what they all seemed to do. He gave the top of my head a shake.

I got another look at Prudhomme as he was leaving the store. He was carrying a flat of beer with one hand up by his shoulder, the way a waiter carries a tray. He slid the case into the front seat of the sedan then got behind the wheel and started the engine. I watched as he lit a cigarette and took a long drag that boiled in his lungs awhile before issuing from his nostrils in fast-moving parallel streams.

"I thought you said football players weren't supposed to smoke?" I said to my father. We were heading home now.

"They're not. Cigarette smoke cuts your wind. Come the fourth quarter, your lungs feel like they're about to explode."

"How about beer? What does that do?"

"Nothing good, either." He seemed to anticipate my next question. "Remi's not thinking straight today, John Ed. He's got a lot of God-given ability, but he must've left his thinking cap back in Kansas City."

We went down the road a ways, headed for Delmas Street. "I don't really like the Chiefs," I said.

"You don't like Lenny Dawson?"

"He's all right, but I don't want to play for Kansas City."

"I don't blame you." He shook his head. "What did you think of Remi's Super Bowl ring?"

"I don't like jewelry, either," I answered.

"Neither do I," said my father, "especially on a man."

✦ ✦ ✦

The earliest indication that I might have a future as a college football player came in the spring of my sophomore year at Opelousas High. The fantasy had long been there, of course, but so few boys from my school received scholarship offers that I was certain I'd never get one. This belief was based on many factors, not the least of which was a strong personal conviction that I wasn't any good.

At six-foot-two and a hundred and eighty-seven pounds, I was hardly the bulky Neanderthal recruiters envision for the center position, and I didn't run particularly well, either. The year before, in a postseason bowl game with a small school from the parish, I replaced the starting center at the beginning of the second half and promptly gave up two sacks. That I gave up no more the rest of the afternoon had nothing to do with my ability to rebound from adversity. Desperate to neutralize a nose guard who threatened to single-handedly wreck our chances to win, head coach Mickey Guidry schemed to have both guards help me out in passing situations. When our quarterback dropped back to throw, three of us were assigned to block one man, and while this left the lanes on either side of me open for blitzing line-backers to exploit, the defense was committed to dropping back to protect against the pass. I got a lucky break that day. Had the other team seized the opportunity and rushed its linebackers, I would've given up more sacks in one half than the average line-man does in his entire high school career.

At season's end, I decided I wanted to be the kind of line-man who blows people off the ball. To gain body mass, I put myself on a diet of my own invention and began to consume carbohydrates in vast quantities—pasta, bread, rice and more pasta, bread and rice. Each night at supper, my mother let me eat as much as I wanted, but the staple of my diet was ice cream. At the K&B drugstore in town, you could buy a half-gallon carton for a dollar. Occasionally the store sold two for the price of one. On those days, I arrived early and loaded a shopping cart with the cube-shaped cartons. I paid for this haul with money I'd saved from cutting grass, picking pecans, and other odd jobs. Peeling back the paper carton like a banana and munching from one end to the other, I often ate an entire half gallon in a single sitting.

I once ate four cartons in twelve hours and never picked up a spoon. "You're gross," my sisters told me.

By spring, I'd grown an inch taller, had gained twenty pounds, and had become more competitive at practice, often in view of the visiting recruiters who watched every move from behind Ray-Bans and the bills of low-riding baseball caps. Our offensive line coach, Madison Firman, liked to put us through a drill called Bull in the Ring. Six players formed a circle around a single man, positioning themselves five yards away. Firman assigned each player on the ring a number then called out the number of the man he wanted to attack the bull. The objective was to drive the bull out of the ring or, in the case of the bull, hold your ground.

Firman occasionally called the numbers of the players standing directly behind the bull. He did this because it was important for a lineman to keep his head on a swivel. The bull ran in place at the center of the ring, pivoting from side to side in anticipation of the next assault. Rarely more than a few seconds separated one strike from the next. The bull took a beating, even when he managed to remain in the ring.

Whenever Firman assigned me the bull position, I concentrated on using the first few hits to send a message to the guys on the ring. I knew better than to rely on just a shoulder or a fore-arm; that got you nowhere. Instead, I braced my neck and speared the charging player under the chin with my helmet. This snapped his head back and took away his bearings. I completed the strike by thrusting forward from my hips and lower body, which was often enough to put the invader out of commission.

Firman liked to send the toughest players after the bull at the end of the drill, and by the time they came running at me, I'd reached a murderous state. Even after all the players in the ring had been vanquished, I continued to run in place, challenging Firman to send more. I moved my body in a tight pivot, ready for any challenge he had to offer. "Who's next?" I yelled, still wearing my mouthpiece. "Send him. Come on, Coach. Send somebody."

By then, I'd learned how to let my mind go, how to escape the practice field, and even as I was handing out and receiving hits, I was at home in an air-conditioned room eating a cube of ice cream in front of the TV. Or at a movie with Denise Landreneau, holding her hand in the dark theater and stealing kisses whenever the action slowed.

Firman had yet one more exercise to test our toughness: a long chute made of iron pipes, standing slightly more than four feet tall and running for a distance of ten yards. Every day Firman had us run from one end of the narrow tunnel to the other. The object was to train yourself to keep your body low to the ground, to strike with more power than you would if you ran tall. Everybody hated the chute. If you lifted your head, you banged your helmet against one of the pipes on the ceiling. The blow knocked you senseless. To make the drill even more difficult, Firman placed boards end to end on the ground to make us widen our stances. Linemen who blocked with their feet too close together had poor balance and virtually no punching power. The boards forced us to keep them shoulder-width apart, which gave us a better base from which to operate.

Players with low centers of gravity had no problem running the chute, but tall guys struggled to keep their balance. I can still feel the *clap clap clap* of my helmet clipping the pipes as I ran, *clap clap clap* as I raced to the opening. Sometimes, for sport, Firman ordered a player to greet you on the other end. The moment you cleared the last pipe, a defensive lineman uncoiled from a four-point stance. You took blows coming and going—the first to your face, the second from a pipe to the back of your head.

Firman liked to hear us growl when we ran drills: Like scores of other state high school teams that wished to emulate LSU, we were nicknamed the Tigers. "Growl," Firman shouted. "Come on. Let me hear you." But it was hard to growl like a Siamese kitten, much less a Bengal tiger, on a muggy Louisiana day when you were exhausted and struggling to breathe; and one afternoon our growls must've sounded puny and insincere. They'd put him in a mood. "Growl for me. Growl, I'm telling you. *Growl!*"

I growled as loud as I could, but as I was leaving the chute Firman cocked a forearm and slammed it against my shoulder. "I told you to growl. That's not growling."

A former college lineman, Firman had maintained a massive upper body, arms dense with muscle, and lean, well-defined legs into his early thirties. He didn't hit me as hard as he could have, but the blow packed enough power to lift me out of one of my shoes. "Hey, son, you growl when I tell you to growl. Let's go."

I looked at him with all the fury I could muster. It was a look meant to communicate a barely controlled desire to kill him and every member of his family.

I slipped my shoe back on and started to run past him when suddenly he grabbed the back of my jersey and pulled me toward him. "Don't look at me like that."

"How did I look at you, Coach?"

He hooked a finger on the bottom rung of my facemask and pulled me closer still. "Don't talk back to me, either. You know better than to talk back to me, John Ed."

"Coach, I didn't mean—"

"What did I just tell you?"

"But Coach—"

The recruiters were watching from under a goalpost about thirty yards away. Worse, my father had witnessed the incident. He was standing on the other side of the chain link fence that separated the field from a campus parking lot. You've shamed him, I thought. Daddy had left coaching several years before to become a school principal, but he still showed up for most practices, drawn less by my role with the team than by habit. Twenty-five years ago, he was the starting center at Opelousas High, now that job belonged to me. He also played linebacker on defense, as I did. Who'd have thought that Johnny Bradley—*Coach* Bradley— would raise a son who got smart and talked back to authority?

Firman blew his whistle, ending the exercise. He ordered us to break the line in half and moved players to the defensive end of the chute. I joined this group, aware that it was an opportunity to unload on someone and redeem myself. I nailed a couple of guys as they left the chute, hitting them with such force that I could feel the air exit their lungs and their weight shift downward when their knees gave out. I glanced over at my father to see his reaction. He gave none. The recruiters didn't seem impressed either.

We were scheduled to move to the main field for a scrimmage, but Firman shouted for us to stay where we were. "Big Hamm," he called out. "Get over there." He was pointing to the chute exit, where I had just been. "John Ed," and now he motioned for me to stand at the entrance.

I considered throwing my helmet at him and sprinting for the showers, even as my teammates began to applaud and pound my shoulder pads. Donald Hammond wasn't like the rest of us. For starters, he was so heavy he eclipsed the three-hundred-and-fifty-pound weight limit on the locker room scale. Players joked that the only way to get the correct reading was to take him to the feed store on Railroad Avenue and put him on a scale used to weigh sacks of beans and corn. When Guidry couldn't find a helmet big enough to fit Hamm, he ordered a shell without any padding from a manufacturer that supplied equipment to the NFL. Even that helmet didn't fit. Big Hamm's face poked out and pressed up flush against the birdcage.

Big Hamm was a nose guard, and it was impossible to move him off the line of scrimmage, even when we double- and triple-teamed him. He lifted guards and centers off their feet and drove them into quarterbacks, then drove the quarterbacks into running backs, then drove the whole pile into the ground. He might've rated as the finest defensive lineman in the history of high school football if only he were effective for more than ten plays a game. He was so big he usually lost his wind after a few series of downs, and after that his night was over. Simply jogging from the sideline to the defensive huddle was enough to exhaust him. He spent the rest of the game recuperating on the bench, an oxygen mask held to his face.

Big Hamm was a hard worker, but Guidry and Firman let him coast through most practices. And Firman inserted him into drills only sparingly, not wishing to hurt anyone, including Hamm himself, who suffered the effects of the weather more than the rest of us. To my recollection, Firman had never put Big Hamm in the defensive position at the end of the chute. It meant suicide for the charging player. I was going to my death, and I knew it as well as everyone else.

"You scared, John Ed?" Firman said.

"I'm not scared."

"What did you say?"

"I'm not scared, *Coach*." I added a growl to prove it.

"He says he's not scared of you, Big Hamm."

Big Hamm smiled and buttoned his chinstrap, and then he lowered himself to a four-point stance. I hesitated a moment before getting in position. By now my teammates, standing all around me, had reached a near hysterical state. They screamed and laughed and threw fists at each other's pads. Players and coaches came running from other parts of the field, many of them letting out war cries. I glanced at the recruiters then over at my father. They stared back with the unflinching stoicism you see on the faces of pallbearers at a military funeral.

"Go on my count," Firman said. "On two . . . " He held an invisible football in front of him, imitating a quarterback who was waiting to receive a snap from center. "Blue seventy-eight," he called. "Blue seventy-eight. Hut *hut*—"

I came blasting out of my stance and hurtling down the chute as fast as I could run, taking short, choppy steps to keep from catching my cleats on the boards and growling with such ferocity that I surely would have impressed a real tiger. My helmet smacked a pipe on the ceiling and gave my neck a jolt, but I continued forward, gaining speed and momentum. Then suddenly I was in the cool and the dark of a movie theater with Denise Landreneau, sharing popcorn and a Coke as we watched Robert Redford and Barbra Streisand in *The Way We Were*. Hubble Gardner was the name of Redford's character, and I recalled how much I disliked my own name, and of course I made a mental note to ask my parents why on earth I had to be called what I'm called when they could've gone with Hubble, and then the movie screen went black as I cleared the last pipe and Big Hamm exploded into me.

He came up from down low and caught me in the exact spot where I myself aimed when I wanted to hurt people—the chin. It seemed he'd crushed my jaw and shattered my teeth even though I was wearing a mouthpiece. The second blow came from behind me, and it was every bit as devastating. Big Hamm had me pinned against the pipes. He pushed through me as he'd been taught to do, aiming his helmet at a spot just behind me. The chute came up off the ground. When I finally came to, half a minute later, it was to the cheers of my teammates.

Firman lifted me off the ground, and I registered the look of surprise and admiration on his face. Each player took a turn slapping my helmet. This was their way of congratulating me, but each slap sent an electric shock from the top of my skull into my left shoulder. The last player to slap my helmet was Big Hamm himself. I dropped to the sod again.

The scrimmage was out of the question. Somebody hoisted me up and walked me to the locker room carrying a good share of my weight. I was deposited on a padded table and our team trainer, Colonel Dudley Tatman, put an ice pack on my tender, stinging neck. When practice ended and the rest of the squad joined me, I was sitting on a metal folding chair in front of my locker, naked but for a jockstrap and the Ace bandages that kept the ice pack in place. I noticed the recruiters watching me from across the room.

My teammates later told me that the collision with Big Hamm sounded like a shotgun blast. I snapped his head back and he staggered a step in reverse before recovering and making his kill.

"You're a brave man," one said. "I want you to remember what I'm telling you today. Are you listening?"

"Yes, I'm listening."

"You're going to play for LSU."

"Get out of here."

"Hey, just remember what I'm telling you."

I was the last player to leave. I'd missed a ride home with my neighbor Timmy Miller, a starting receiver on the team. Guidry offered to drop me off, but when we walked outside I saw my father's pickup waiting under a streetlight in the parking lot. He himself was leaning against the old heap as a cloud of insects flew in the hot, yellow air above him. Cold water from the ice pack drained down my back and settled in the seat of my pants as I limped to the passenger side and let myself in.

"Thank you, Mickey," my father called out.

"Good to see you again, Coach."

Each gave the other a wave and Guidry secured the locker

room door. I was looking back at coach in the side-view mirror, waiting for my father to start for home, when he cupped his mouth with his hands. "Hey, Coach Bradley," he shouted.

My father wheeled around and brought a hand to his ear.

"John Ed's going to be one hell of a football player."

We started down Judson Walsh Drive, passing under the heavy branches of pine and oak trees that lined the road and formed a tunnel, each of us holding an arm out his open window. The air smelled of evergreen mixed with honeysuckle and gardenia from the old Humble Village neighborhood that had been abandoned decades before and now stood black and overgrown, a ghost town on the side of the road. I wanted to go to my room, get in bed, and hide under the covers until I was so old that the day had been erased from the memories of everyone who witnessed it. My father hooked a right onto the Old Sunset Road. He started working through the gears, and by the time he reached third I couldn't keep a lid on it anymore. "I hate it," I said, stuff leaking in a torrent from my nose. "I hate it, I tell you. I hate it, I hate it . . ."

There was a smile on his face. He reached over and felt the ice pack to make sure it was still cold. "You hate it? You hate football?"

"Yes, I hate football."

He was quiet for a time, and I looked at him in the light of the dashboard. "You want to quit?" he asked.

"Yes, sir."

He nodded, keeping his eyes on the road. "Well, if that's what you want you can call Coach Guidry and Coach Firman in

the morning and let them know. When we get home, you can tell
your mother. You can tell your brothers and sisters too."

"I didn't say I was going to quit. I said I *wanted* to quit."

"Then I'm mistaken?"

"Yes, sir."

"You won't need to call your coaches?"

"No."

"No what?"

"No, sir."

He parked in front of the house and killed the engine. I
could see Mama at the kitchen window and behind her Donna
on the phone. A year ahead of me at school, Donna was a cheer-
leader and one of the most popular girls in her class. No one was
prouder than she of my place on the team. Now Bobby entered
the picture, standing on his tiptoes to look out the window and
see who'd pulled up out front. He vanished and a few seconds
later I spotted him at the door, waiting to find out how practice
went, to check my arms and legs for new cuts and bruises, evidence of collisions with teammates.

At that moment I understood something that I was sure my
father had realized long ago. There comes a time when quitting
stops being an option, when quitting means quitting on those
who are counting on you and quitting on your destiny, and
although I was still groggy from Big Hamm's hit, I understood
this with absolute clarity. It was too late now to quit the team. It
would always be too late.

My father never wore a hat in the house. He took his cap off. "I don't want to make you think you have to play," he said. "Everybody gets knocked down. Not everybody gets up, though. Today you got up."

"You don't need to tell me that. It would be better if you didn't say anything." I pushed the door open and stepped outside. "What'd Mama cook for supper?"

"Mixed meat and rice and gravy."

"I hate mixed meat."

"When you're done eating, you're going to thank her and tell her how good it was. You hear me, boy?"

"Yes, sir."

He took his time walking around to my side of the truck, and together we started under the pine trees for the house. I wasn't feeling any better, so he held me by the elbow and made sure I didn't drift.

John Ed Bradley is the author of several highly praised novels, including Tupelo Nights *and* My Juliet. *A former staff writer for* The Washington Post, *Bradley has contributed feature stories to* Sports Illustrated, Esquire, *and* GQ. It Never Rains in Tiger Stadium *was published in 2007. Bradley lives in the historic Coliseum Square in New Orleans' Lower Garden District.*

After Jackie

--- ✦ ---

HENRY AARON
AS TOLD TO CAL FUSSMAN

I can remember being a kid back in Mobile sitting on the back porch when an airplane flew over. I told my father when I grew up I was going to be a pilot. You know what he said? He said, "Ain't no colored pilots."

So I told him I'd be a ballplayer. And he said, "Ain't no colored ballplayers."

There were a lot of things blacks couldn't be back then. There weren't any colored pilots. There weren't any colored ballplayers in the major leagues. So it was hard to have those dreams.

Then Jackie came with the Brooklyn Dodgers to Mobile for an exhibition game in 1948. I went to hear him talk to a crowd in front of a drugstore. I skipped school to meet Jackie Robinson. If it were on videotape, you'd probably see me standing there with my mouth wide open.

I don't remember what he said. It didn't matter what he said. *He was standing there.*

My father took me to see Jackie play in that exhibition game. After that day, he never told me ever again that I couldn't be a ballplayer.

I was allowed to dream after that.

Cal Fussman is a writer for ESPN The Magazine *and* Esquire. *He has interviewed Jimmy Carter, Robert DeNiro, Jack Welch, Muhammad Ali, General Tommy Franks, Robert McNamara, Donald Trump, Ted Kennedy, Sumner Redstone, George Steinbrenner, Jeff Bezos, Al Pacino, and Rudy Giuliani, to name a few. He lives with his family in Chapel Hill, N.C.*

Pistol: The Life of Pete Maravich

◆

MARK KRIEGEL

They cannot see him, this slouching, ashen-faced man in their midst. To their oblivious eyes, he remains what he once was, unblemished by the years, much as he appeared on his first bubblegum card: a halo of hair, the fresh-faced, sad-eyed wizard cradling a grainy leather orb.

One of the regulars, a CPA, retrieved that very card last night. He found it in a shoe box, tucked away with an old train set and a wooden fort in a crawl space in his parents' basement.

He brought it to the gym this morning to have it signed or, in some way, sanctified. The 1970 rookie card of Pete Maravich, to whom the Atlanta Hawks had just awarded the richest contract in professional sports, takes note of the outstanding facts: that Maravich was coached by his father, under whose tutelage he became "the most prolific scorer in the history of college basketball." Other salient statistics are provided in agate type: an average of 44.2 points a game, a total of 3,667 (this when nobody else had scored 3,000). The records will never be broken. Still, they are woefully inadequate in measuring the contours of the Maravich myth.

Maravich wasn't an archetype; he was several: child prodigy, prodigal son, his father's payment in a Faustian bargain. He was a creature of contradictions, ever alone: the white hope of a black sport, a virtuoso stuck in an ensemble, an exuberant showman who couldn't look you in the eye, a vegetarian boozer, the athlete who lived like a rock star, a profligate, suicidal genius saved by Jesus Christ.

Still, it's his caricature that evokes unqualified affection in men of a certain age. Pistol Pete, they called him. The Pistol is another relic of the '70s, not unlike bongs and Bruce Lee flicks: the skinny kid who mesmerized the basketball world with Globetrotters moves, floppy socks and great hair.

But above all, Pistol Pete was his father's vision, built to the old man's exacting specifications. And the game now in progress is a dance in deference to that patrimony. The squeak of sneakers against the floor produces an odd chirping melody. Then there's another rhythm, the respiration of men well past their prime, an assortment of white guys: the accountant, insurance salesmen, financial planners, even a preacher. "Just a bunch of duffers," recalls one.

"Fat old men," smirks another.

But they play as if Pistol Pete, or what's left of him, could summon the boys they once were. They acknowledge him with a superfluous flourish, an extra behind-the-back pass or an unnecessary between-the-legs dribble. The preacher, a gentle-voiced man of great renown in evangelical circles, reveals a feverishly competitive nature. After hitting a shot, he bellows, "You get that on camera?"

The Parker Gymnasium at the First Church of the Nazarene in Pasadena could pass for a good high school gym— a clean, cavernous space with arching wooden rafters and large windows. At dawn, its halogen lamps give off a glow to the outside world, a beacon to spirits searching for a game. As a boy, Maravich would have considered this a kind of heaven. Now it's a way station of sorts.

Pete begins wearily. He hasn't played in a long time, and he moves at one-quarter speed, if that. He does not jump; he shuffles. The ball seems like a shot-put shot in his hands; on his second attempt at the basket it barely touches the front of the rim. But gradually, as the pace of his breath melds with that of the others and he starts to sweat, Pete Maravich recovers something in himself. "The glimpse of greatness was in his ball handling," the accountant will recall. "There would just be some kind of dribble or something. Just the quickness of the beat." There was genius in that unexpected cadence, a measure of music. The Pistol's talent, now as then, was musical. He was as fluent as Mozart, but he was sold like Elvis, the white guy performing in a black idiom. And for a time, he was mad like Elvis too.

Now the accountant tries to blow past Pete with a nifty spin move. Pete tells him not to believe his own hype. The Pistol wears an easy grin. Moments later he banks one in.

That smile again. What a goof.

The game ends. Guys trudge off to the water fountain. Pete continues to shoot around. And now you wonder what he sees.

Is it as he used to imagine? "The space will open up," he once said. "Beyond that will be heaven, and when you go inside, then the space closes again and you are there ... definitely a wonderful place ... Everyone you ever knew will be there."

The preacher asks Pete Maravich how he feels.

"I feel great," he says.

In the next moment Pete begins to sway. Then his eyes roll back. The sound of his head hitting the floor will haunt those within earshot. Pete has begun to foam at the mouth. The preacher holds his head, trying to keep Pete from swallowing his tongue. He and another player administer CPR. Next, the EMS crew takes its turn. As the medics work, shooting jolts of electricity through his torso, the players kneel in prayer.

God's will be done, they say.

Why now? they ask.

Finally, what remains of Pete Maravich is taken away in a slow-moving ambulance. No siren.

After returning from World War II, Press Maravich spent a season playing for the Pittsburgh Ironmen in what would be regarded as the inaugural year of the NBA. It was 1947, and the league wanted young men fresh out of college. There wasn't much of a market for a thirty-three-year-old guard who had spent his best years as a Navy fighter pilot. Press's preposterous idea that one could make a living playing basketball had run its course.

But in the death of that dream lay the genesis of another. A friend would recall the night Press barged in at halftime of a semipro game—"one of those games where you're lucky to get a chipped-ham sandwich and a fishbowl of beer"—and announced, "My wife had a boy." This boy would do what his father could not; his body language would articulate the old man's vanity, genius, ambition. Eventually he would surpass even his father's imagination. On June 24, 1947, a Serbian Orthodox priest from St. Elijah the Prophet came to the Maravich home on Beech Wood Avenue in Aliquippa, Pa. The baby was baptized Peter Press.

By 1950 Press was coaching basketball and teaching phys ed at Aliquippa High School, where he himself had been a hoops legend. A new sheriff had come to the blackboard jungle, confiscating 300 switchblades and paddling students who violated his vaunted rules. "It was a piece of wood, three or four inches wide—[Press] was pretty loose with that paddle," recalls Nick Lackovich, then a student at Aliquippa.

Press had become a hard-ass. The dashing pilot with movie-star looks now wore his hair shorn to bristles. Detesting the duck's ass haircut, Press formed the Crewcut Club. "If you didn't belong, you couldn't play ball for him," says Pete Suder, one of his players.

"Press would run us like crazy, up and down the steps, around the gymnasium," said Mike Ditka, then an underclassman, who'd go on to fame as an NFL tight end and the coach of the Chicago Bears. "He'd put that steely look on you, and you knew he meant business."

Not every player saw Press as a mere authority figure. Joe Lee, his star point guard, recalls him with deep affection. Lee was black, as was half the Aliquippa team by then. His mother had passed away, and even by Aliquippa standards Joe Lee was poor. Press would often slip him lunch tickets. More than that, though, Press showed a level of concern Lee had not seen in other adults.

Press took his team all the way to Madison Square Garden in New York City because he wanted the boys to see firsthand that their game had a capital and, within it, a cathedral. On Sundays during the season he would drive them to Duquesne University to watch the varsity practice. On the way he would listen to the black radio station. Press knew all the words to the spirituals.

"That's your heritage," he told Lee, who found Press to be a surprisingly good listener. Once, Lee asked his coach why Aliquippa had no black cheerleaders. Press thought about it for a while. "You're right," he said. "There should be."

Press's Aliquippa teams also had their own mascot. He had sad, soft eyes and a big head mounted on a wispy frame. He was tiny but ubiquitous. If you saw Press, you saw Pete. He attended practices. He'd wiggle his way into team huddles. At home games, Suder recalls, "he'd sit on the bench right next to his dad."

"He always wanted to be around Press," says Joe Pukach, then Press's assistant, "but Press was always around basketball."

Woody Sauldsberry, a Globetrotter from 1955 through '57, remembers proud Papa Press bringing Pete into the locker room when the team played in Pittsburgh. "His father knew some of the older players," recalls Sauldsberry. "He would bring Pete in the dressing room, and the guys would take time with him. They would do some ball-handling tricks. Then he would do some. I remember he could dribble the ball down stairs. The kid was only seven or eight years old, but you could tell he was going to be good."

"That's all [Press] talked about: his son, his son, his son," says Suder. "Press pushed him like crazy." Suder also recalls that the coach, unlike many steelworker fathers, "had his arms around him all the time." The game was an obsession, but also a kind of love. Press worshipped basketball. Pete worshipped Press.

On the afternoons of away games, the team would meet at four o'clock in the gym before riding out in the bus. Press would leave Pete behind with the lights on and this instruction: "Play." When the team returned to Aliquippa, usually between midnight and one in the morning, Pete would still be there, still shooting.

In 1955 Press took the head job at Clemson, becoming the basketball coach at a football school. His job was to be a good loser to the ACC powerhouses, North Carolina, N.C. State, Wake Forest and Duke. Shortly after he was hired he said, "We expect Clemson to play interesting basketball . . . basketball that the fans like to see."

Interesting basketball. At a place like Clemson, Press's coaching acumen couldn't be judged in wins and losses. Lacking a player capable of art, he conducted experiments in basketball science. Some were crazy, others brilliant. One was both: the grand experiment, a supremely interesting player, a product of talent and desire, an expression of his father's imagination, a boy by whom one could judge the man.

As a coach's coach, Press loved nothing more than entertaining other members of the fraternity at the Maravich house. They'd talk basketball as they sipped coffee and nibbled on cake. Then they'd adjourn for the main event. "He was dying to show off little Pete," recalls Bill Hensley, then the sports information director at N.C. State. "We would go down to the basement, and Pete would dribble for us on the concrete floor." The kid could dribble like Bob Cousy. "Then Press would put gloves on him so he couldn't feel the ball." The kid still dribbled like Cousy—and then some. Pete would be going between his legs, behind his legs, throwing it against the wall, catching it behind his back. He was a machine.

Finally, Hensley recalls, Press would produce a handkerchief. "He would blindfold Pete so he couldn't see the ball." Never saw Cousy do that. Never saw anyone do that. "Before or since," says Hensley. "We'd sit there for like half an hour, watching this little bitty kid dribbling everywhere. We felt then that Press might have something special on his hands." That was during the 1956–57 season. Pete was nine.

Before long he was making the rounds with his father on the summer circuit. Their big stop was the Campbell College basketball camp in Buies Creek, N.C. For years Press roomed there with UCLA coach John Wooden. They were an odd couple: Wooden measured and modest, Press loud and profane. "Press was an enigma," Wooden says of his cussing colleague. "I came to understand that it was just his way. But he knew the Bible so well."

Not as well as he knew basketball, of course. "One should never underestimate Press's knowledge of the game," says Wooden. "Over the years he was the one I would go to for analysis on several aspects of the game." At UCLA, Wooden would become the most successful coach in basketball history. He would win ten national championships and coach nineteen first-team All-Americas. Press never got to work with that kind of talent. He had only Pete.

Wooden first saw Pete around 1960. The boy was performing the dribbling and ball-handling routines that would become so famous. "I saw him do things at Campbell I didn't think anybody could do," Wooden says flatly. In assessing the boy's talent and dexterity the coach compares him to some of the great black players he had known, going back to his days as an All-America at Purdue: "I had the great pleasure of playing against the New York Rens many times. They had some of the best ballplayers you could ever see. I watched the Globetrotters with Goose Tatum and Marques Haynes. None of them could do more than Pete. Pete Maravich could do more with a basketball than anybody I have ever seen."

Then again, Wooden felt obligated to ask his enigmatic friend, To what end? All those tricks, what did they accomplish? "It's crazy," he said. "How many hours does it take to learn all that? Wouldn't he be better off learning proper footwork for defense?"

"You don't understand," said Press. "He's going to be the first million-dollar pro."

The gloves and blindfolds were just the beginning. There were so many other drills. Pete learned the fundamentals, of course: dribbling with either hand, chest pass, bounce pass, foul shots, jump shots and hook shots. But because the basics could become monotonous, Press invented more elaborate regimens. Most of these moves were anathema to coaches of the day, but they kept Pete's interest alive. Often the ideas came to Press in his sleep.

In all there were about forty drills and exercises—Homework Basketball, they would come to be called. Press and Pete gave each of them a name, such as Pretzel, Ricochet, Crab Catch, Flap Jack, or Punching Bag. Pete would crouch, his arms moving in a figure-eight motion between and around his legs so rapidly that the ball looked as if it were suspended beneath him. He would bounce the ball two-handed between his splayed legs, catch it behind his back and then fire it forward, completing the pendulum motion. He would transform himself into a kind of human gyroscope. The beat of the ball as he dribbled it just inches from the ground approximated the staccato sound of a boxing speed bag. Perfected at Pete's pace, the drills had an almost hypnotic effect.

Pete would dribble the two miles between his home and College Avenue, the town's main drag. He'd dribble while riding his bicycle—alternating hands. One day Press told his son to get in the car and bring his ball. Pete did as he was told. Then Press instructed him to lie across the backseat with the passenger-side door open. Pete balked. He said, "What are people going to think?"

"Just do it," said Press.

Pete did it. He dribbled as his father drove, learning to control the ball at different speeds.

He'd also dribble in the movie theater, keeping time on the carpeted aisle through a double feature. He'd dribble in Martin's Drugstore, where he once won a five-dollar bet by spinning the ball on his fingertips for an hour straight.

Years later, Maravich would famously declare his childhood self "a basketball android." But androids don't think or feel, and the ball was an appendage not merely of his body but of his psyche as well. He went to bed with it, lulling himself to sleep while practicing his shooting form. He would repeat the words "fingertip control, backspin, follow-through" like a mantra. For Pete, there was comfort in repetition. Still, he was a light sleeper, as was his father. Once Pete awoke in a driving rainstorm. "I forced open my bedroom window and crawled out into the downpour," he would recall in his autobiography. "In my bare feet I ran to the muddied ground and began to dribble . . . I knew if I could dribble under these conditions, I would have no problem on a basketball court."

Frail as he looked, Pete didn't acknowledge the usual boundaries of fatigue, age or nerve. Nor did his routines distinguish between the athletic and the aesthetic, between sport and show. He had already begun challenging his father's players to games of H-O-R-S-E for money. He would have to hoist the ball two-handed, off his hip. "He was half our size, literally," remembers George Krajack. "But he took some of our guys' money."

At Campbell, Pete bet Wake Forest's All-America big man, Len Chappell, that he could make twenty-four of twenty-five free throws, with twenty of them hitting nothing but the net. He collected his winnings in Pepsis. In getting the better of Chappell, Pete had done something the rest of the ACC could not. It wasn't the only time, either. "I remember we played H-O-R-S-E for an hour," says Chappell. "He shot me out of the gym."

"He was the hardest-working athlete I've ever been around," says Lefty Driesell, then the coach at Davidson. "It'd be 110 degrees, and he'd be dribbling or throwing the ball against a cement wall hours at a time."

"Pete," Driesell told him, "you're working too hard."

"I'm gonna be a millionaire, coach," Pete replied. The boy kept going, throwing all those fancy passes against the wall.

"I ain't never seen Oscar Robertson throw nothing but a plain old chest pass," said Driesell.

"They don't pay you a million to throw a plain old chest pass."

While still at Clemson, Press developed ulcers. Basketball was literally bleeding him. His physician prescribed tranquilizers and advised Press not to take the game home with him.

"How can I do that?" Press asked. The real cure, at least to his way of thinking, was Pete. This Pistol had the magic bullet: a cure for all his regrets. Pete was Press's ticket to basketball heaven. Still, some couldn't help but wonder whether Pete would become a kind of human sacrifice. As John Wooden had warned Press, "You're putting too much pressure on one boy."

By 1965 Press had become the head coach at a bona fide basketball school, North Carolina State. There, he guided an undermanned Wolfpack team to an ACC championship and a ticket to the NCAA tournament, where its first opponent would be Princeton, a team made famous by its star, Bill

Bradley. A first team All-America, Bradley had won a gold medal in Rome, where he was captain of the U.S. Olympic team, and a Rhodes scholarship. The AP, UPI, and Basketball Writers Association would all name him college basketball's player of the year. In three varsity seasons he had averaged more than thirty points a game. But even more significant was the manner in which he scored. "We knew," recalls '65 Wolfpack star Pete Coker, "that a different style was being created in places like New York, Washington and Philly." A new game was developing; segregation could no longer keep it secret. But Bradley represented a triumph, however perishable, of the old style.

Here, then, was a Great White Hope. And more. Bradley personified the ideal collegiate athlete. His game was modest, practiced, even Protestant. Not only did he belong to the Fellowship of Christian Athletes, but he also taught Sunday school. Bradley, for whom khakis and white shirts were a standard-issue uniform, had made an art of conformity. "We were mesmerized by [him]," says Les Robinson, one of Press's seniors, recalling the Wolfpack's deflating rout by the Ivy Leaguers, 66–48, including twenty-seven points from Bradley. "Press showed me film of the game the next day . . . We weren't guarding him like we guarded other guys. That's what killed Press, that we were in awe of him."

With the exception of that loss, it had been a wonderful season, proof of what Press could do at a basketball school. He was voted the ACC's coach of the year, but the most convincing evidence of his aptitude—and his outrageous aspiration for changing the game—wasn't an award but a performance. It had taken place earlier that season, over the Christmas break, at Reynolds Coliseum. Only a half-dozen guys were there, but Bill Bradley himself inspired only a fraction of the awe they felt that day.

The game was three-on-three. There were four N.C. State starters: Coker, Larry Lakins, Larry Worsley and Tommy Mattocks. There was Robinson. Pete made six. He was seventeen.

"We loved to play against Pete," Lakins would recall. "He was the coach's son. Coach worked our tails off. That was our only retaliation." They bellied him. They shoved him. They hit him. "We were beating the s— out of him that day," says Coker.

But none of that punishment made a difference. Whatever Pete threw up came down through the net. There were jump shots, hook shots, set shots, bank shots, left- and righthanded shots, driving shots and shots that seemed to come all the way from Guilford County. The game went on for hours as each player took his turn trying to guard Pete. None of them could.

By then Robinson had an idea of how good the kid was; they would play one-on-one most Saturdays. But he had never seen Pete as he was that day: the way he taunted starters on an ACC championship team, teasing them with that high yo-yo dribble. And then, as soon as one of them leaned or lunged, he was embarrassed; Pete was gone.

Bradley was hypnotically economical. Pete was his stylistic antithesis. Everything about this boy's game was funky and flagrant. He went behind the back, over the back, between his legs, between your legs. Then there was that pass with English on it, the one that bounced off the floor at an absurd angle. Years later a basketball writer would liken the ball's movement to something that came off a pool hustler's cue. But the sense of timing suggested an accomplished comedian.

As the game wound down, toward the end of its third hour, Pete invented a shot. He was fading to a corner. The stairs down to the dressing room were just beyond the court. "Going down," Pete called as he threw up a high, arcing hook shot. He didn't even break his stride, didn't stop to watch it swish though the net. He just kept going, right on down to the locker room.

Coker and Robinson ambled over to the bench and sat, speechless, shaking their heads. Finally, Coker spoke: "Les, you ever see anything like that?"

Robinson shook his head no.

Coker said, "I think he might be . . . "

Robinson was nodding now.

" . . . might be the best who ever was."

Working at the edge of art and science, father and son produced a kind of vaudeville. "Showtime," they called it. They had come as a package deal to LSU, another football school, in 1966, and they toured the state of Louisiana, hitting towns like Shreveport and Alexandria, enticing the people, provoking their gossip, selling them on Tigers basketball. Each LSU player had his own Homework Basketball drill to perform as a specialty. But the main attraction—nay, the only attraction—was Pete. "Pete was an advertising campaign," says Bud Johnson, the LSU publicity man.

No one was more susceptible to the charms of his game than kids. Suddenly, in the heart of football country, sporting goods stores couldn't stock enough basketballs, hoops, and nets. And back in North Carolina, teenagers like Charlotte's M.L. Carr—one of the first blacks to attend the basketball camp at Campbell—were rehearsing Pete's Homework Basketball routines until they could do them in their sleep. "I knew I couldn't be like Pete," says Carr. "But I did every drill religiously."

At sixteen, Carr had a sense of the game and its stylistic antecedents. He knew about Earl (the Pearl) Monroe from Winston-Salem State Teachers College, author of the spin dribble. He knew of Providence's Jimmy Walker and his famous crossover, a change-of-hands dribble that made the quickest defenders look slow. Then there was Archie Clark of Minnesota, who had perfected the stutter step, a hesitation move. "But Pete," says Carr, "was the best I'd ever seen. He did things the Globetrotters couldn't do yet."

In fact, Pete was already being called "a bleached Globetrotter." But unlike the Globetrotters, he made his moves in authentic game conditions. The competition was high level, high stakes, the expectations increasing at an exponential rate.

With his droopy socks and floppy hair, there was a growing sense that Pistol Pete would morph into something more iconic than just a basketball player. In anticipation of his varsity debut, in 1967, Press saw to it that LSU had a new pep band and a squadron of pom-pom girls. He arranged to videotape Pete's games and the Homework Basketball drills. There would be a full record of exactly how he and his son had conspired to change the game.

By Press's calculation Pete would have to shoot forty times a game for LSU to have a chance of winning. Not only did this theory violate every strategic principle of the game, but it also had never been put into practice. Shooting at such an absurdly rapid rate—better than a shot a minute—would be physically and psychologically grueling. "He's got more pressure on him than any kid in America," Press said.

Pete's game became the subject of discussion among league officials. Coming down full stride on the break, he would wave his hand over the ball, then tip it with the other hand in the opposite direction. It looked like a magic trick. At one point a ref blew his whistle and signaled a traveling violation. "How can you make that call?" said an outraged Pete. "You've never even seen that move."

In fact, the call forced SEC officials to hold a meeting. The refs examined the tape until, at long last, they shook their heads in grudging agreement with the kid.

Suddenly, calling LSU games had become a complicated proposition. Officials had to rethink the game as it pertained to the league's new sensation. "One thing you didn't want to do was foul [Pete] out of the game," says Charlie Bloodworth, a veteran SEC official. "Pete put more people in the seats than anybody."

Fan mail arrived at the LSU athletic department by the sackful. Practices became targets of opportunity for groupies and autograph seekers. Pete's practice socks were pilfered from the trainer's laundry bags. That's when Pete started washing them himself. Those socks were talismans; teenage boys began to abuse their own white hosiery until it was acceptably gray and droopy. And this was in football country. Reporters from Georgia and Mississippi who had never even been to a basketball game started making themselves seen. Suddenly, games in places like Oxford and Athens and Tuscaloosa were selling out.

Even the opposing players couldn't take their eyes off Pete. "You were never supposed to look at your opponent during warmups," says Johnny Arthurs, then a high-scoring forward for Tulane. "But there we were: watching Pete put on a show."

Arthurs also recalls watching game film of Pete: "[He] had a move where he got out on the break and dribbled between his legs and then behind his back. We made the coach replay it again and again and again because no one believed he actually did it."

Every so often an amazed Bud Johnson would ask, "Hey, Pete, how come I never saw you practice that one?"

"Oh, yes, I have," Pete would say. "Many times."

"When?"

"In my head."

For Press these moments of basketball genius were the sacred seconds, a synthesis of conceptual art and performance art. As he told Time during that 1967–68 season, "I get to the point where I don't coach him. I just watch."

In Pete's first season of varsity ball, LSU improved from 3–23 to 14–12 while violating the game's every orthodoxy, not to mention the very principles that had made Press—proponent of ensemble basketball, erstwhile defensive guru—a great coach in the first place. Though Pete had long arms and great anticipation, the physical tools of a great defender, he couldn't be bothered with defense. "Pete had to work so damn hard on offense," says starting guard Rich Hickman, "he used defense to rest."

Once again Wooden chalked it up to the enigma of Press. "If any of my players made a behind-the-back pass," says Wooden, "he'd be sitting on the bench. Same thing with the dunk. I didn't permit any of that." (In fact, the NCAA voted to outlaw the dunk in 1967, a move considered a sanction against UCLA's Lew Alcindor. But in a larger sense it was a sanction against a still-emerging black style of basketball.)

The Pistol was featured in Time and Newsweek. Around the same time there was a photo spread in Life and a cover story in SI that served as a chorus of "Auld Lang Syne" for Bill Bradley and all he represented: The Prince is dead; long live the Pistol. Meanwhile, LSU basketball remained a one-man show. By the end of Pete's junior season—Saturday, March 8, 1969—the Tigers needed a win just to break even on the season.

They were in Athens, Georgia, down 59–44 with ten minutes to play. Then, without warning, a mere game became something "seldom matched in SEC basketball," according to an account in the *Baton Rouge State-Times*. Pete scored thirteen straight points and twenty-four of his team's last twenty-nine, most of them on outrageously long jumpers. The game went into overtime. "The crowd starts cheering," says Les Robinson, who was watching from a seat near the LSU bench. "They don't care who wins. They came to see a show."

As the extra period ended, Georgia had a two-point lead and was trying to run out the clock. "Then I heard something I never heard before or since," says Robinson. "The crowd started booing the home team. The players didn't understand. It discombobulated them."

Georgia took an ill-advised shot with twelve seconds remaining. Six ticks later, Maravich tied the game again.

The second overtime proved less competitive but even more memorable, with Pete scoring eleven of LSU's twelve points as the Tigers took an insurmountable lead. "Our place sat, like, 11,000, but there must have been 13,000 in there," says Georgia's Herb White, who had already fouled out trying to guard Pete. "The fans were going nuts. You could not hear anything." Pete might as well have been conducting a dribbling clinic. "Our guys are running around after him, falling down on the floor," White continues.

"He's going into his whole Marques Haynes Globetrotters act, and we can't even catch the sumbitch to foul him."

"They had fire in their eyes," Pete would remember. "I thought they were going to kill me. I started dribbling to mid-court, then to my bench." There were just seconds left. Pete never even broke stride as he threw up a shot for his fifty-seventh and fifty-eighth points on the night. "A thirty-foot hook shot over his head," as it was described in one newspaper account. "The ball hit the bottom of the net without touching the rim of the basket."

"Our cheerleaders started dancing," says White, "then the fans came pouring out of the stands and carried him off the floor."

"They were going after him like Elvis Presley," Robinson remembers. "They just wanted to touch him." Of course, Les had seen it before, the outrageously nonchalant parabola of his final shot: the going-down shot. Robinson caught up with Pete in the dressing room after the game. Middle of winter, and the kid came out in sunglasses.

He hugged Robinson. For once Pete was in awe of himself. "Les," he whispered, "I think it's the greatest game I've ever played."

Soon after Pete Maravich collapsed during that pickup game in Pasadena in 1988, the phone rang in Covington, La. Joshua Maravich, then five years old, heard the maid let out a piercing howl. Then he was quickly ushered into another room.

He closed the door behind him and considered himself in the mirror. He had his father's eyes. That's what everyone said. The boy looked through himself, and he knew: My daddy's dead.

Pete's older son, eight-year-old Jaeson, knew something was amiss when a teacher found him in the school cafeteria. "You need to go home now," she said. The living room was crowded with grown-ups by the time Jaeson arrived. His mother, who had been crying in the corner, got up as he came through the door. She hugged him tight. "I knew it was going to be real bad," he says.

She told him; then he went to his room. He felt nothing. He pulled up the blinds and stared out the window. Five minutes passed. Or was it ten? He does not know. "When I finally figured out that he wasn't coming back, I started to cry," he says.

The next day, in an act that stretched the limits of an eight-year-old's capacity for bravery and observance, Jaeson practiced with his rec league team, the Little Pistols.

In 1996, to celebrate its first fifty years, the NBA enlisted a panel to name the fifty greatest players in its history. A half century had passed since Press Maravich played for the Pittsburgh Ironmen. The NBA, under commissioner David Stern, was now held up as the ideal professional sports enterprise. Stern's model, as he often stated, wasn't another league but rather the savagely synergistic Disney Corporation. Instead of selling Mickey, Minnie and Snow White, the NBA was marketing the greatest athletes in team sports, most of them Americans of African descent.

It was Pete Maravich, however, who had anticipated what the game would become: a hip-hop ballet, a rapper's delight, and a cause for great celebration in the corporate suite. Pistol Pete anticipated the high-concept ballplayer. This was the star identifiable merely as Magic or Charles or, most of all, Michael, an athlete who could be reconstituted in a variety of media, who could play as easily with animated characters as he could on the street.

Of those fifty greatest, Pete was the only one who would have fared better in the contemporary game than when he actually played. This much was now accepted as gospel: Pete had been well ahead of his time. "If he was playing today," said Walt Frazier, one of the chosen fifty, "he'd be the most popular player in the league."

He was also the only one of the 50 not still alive. In his place Jaeson and Josh attended the 1997 All-Star game in Cleveland, where they accepted the honor on their father's behalf. As they awaited their introductions in the tunnel at Gund Arena, the game's greatest fawned over the brothers Maravich. Isiah Thomas told them how much he had learned from watching their father. Magic Johnson, whose championship Los Angeles Lakers teams had appropriated the term Showtime, felt a need to correct the record.

"Your pops," he gushed, "he was the original. He was the real Showtime."

Mark Kriegel, a former sports columnist for the New York Daily News, *is the author of the critically acclaimed best-seller* Namath: A Biography. *He lives in Santa Monica, with his daughter, Holiday.*

Someone You Want to Play With

◆

JEFF BRADLEY

I n the spring of 1985, Jack Nicklaus walked into my room at the Chi Phi fraternity house in Chapel Hill, N.C., and offered to teach me the game of golf.

Okay, not that Jack Nicklaus, the Golden Bear, the winner of 18 major championships, the living legend. It was his son Jack Nicklaus Jr., also known as Jackie, who was a fraternity brother of mine and a class ahead of me at the University of North Carolina. That was the spring I gave up trying to play baseball for the Tar Heels, realizing that, at 5'6" and without a lick of speed, I would never get over the hump and be a varsity player. Why it took me two and a half years to figure this out remains a mystery. But in 1985, my athletic career was over and Jackie recognized my depression. "Come on, we'll go hit some balls," he said. "You can have these clubs. Keep them." He was handing over what looked to be a set of clubs that had been, as they say, gently used. Jack was a player on the Carolina golf team, so I'm sure they were top-of-the-line.

Nonetheless, I said, "Nah. I've got no interest in golf. Not for me."

Jackie pushed the sticks toward me. "Here, take them," he said. "I'll show you the basics, and you can take your time learning. This isn't baseball. You can play this game the rest of your life."

I just waved him off. I'd tried to hit golf balls before, as a kid. My dad bought me a set of junior clubs, got me involved in a clinic at the country club, and all I can remember is that he told me I had a "great swing" as I shanked, topped, and skulled one ball after another. I remember that poorly struck iron shots stung worse than hitting a baseball off the handle on a freezing cold day. Those were my golf memories.

So I turned down a free lesson with Jackie Nicklaus, but what's funny is that a year later, when I was a senior, some of my other fraternity brothers coerced me into taking golf as a physical education class. I then spent a good bit of my final semester of college tearing up the turf at the university golf course. We snuck beers on the course, gambled a bit, surely never broke 100, but had some fun. And then, soon after that, it was off to work.

I didn't touch a golf club for the next four or five years, but when a change of jobs landed me back at my parents house—at the age of 27—my father, who was nearing retirement, asked me one day to go out and play. I took him up on it, and even though I was horrendous, I started to enjoy the game. We played again and again.

A round of golf with my dad became a weekly—sometimes twice weekly—event. Having learned the game when he caddied as a boy, Dad did not give a whole lot of instruction. He never tried to change my grip or my stance. "Hit down on the ball" was about as technical as he would ever get. "Forget the bad shots," he'd always say. "And try to remember the good ones."

Golf changed us. When I brought childhood friends along, for the first time I didn't care if they called him by his first name. My father emerged as a regular guy from the fog of old family relationships. In face, he was a great guy. He wasn't a great player—probably a 14 handicap in his best days—but what I learned from him on the course was something I still try to remember when I play golf today, 20 years later. "Being a good player," he told me, "is not as important as being someone people want to play with."

I've thought of that expression so many times as my love affair with golf has grown, and as my own sons have taken up the game. With one son, who was breaking 90 at the age of 11, and to another, who's struggling with the game, I always stress the same thing, that when they're playing in a group, they need to compliment everyone's game and not just focus on their own. I remind them to do the little things, like saying "Nice shot" when a brother makes solid contact. Or when their grandfather holes a long putt. Typically, the good player has a more difficult time with that issue than the other guy.

We've got a foursome now. Me, my dad, and my two sons. Turns out the present I didn't accept from Jack Nicklaus' son—the pleasures of golf—has become one of the greatest gifts I've been able to give to my own. And to my dad. And I look forward to the day when my sons' buddies tee it up with us, and call me by my first name.

Jeff Bradley is a senior writer for ESPN The Magazine. *He lives at the Jersey Shore with his wife Linda and his sons, Tyler and Beau. Jeff spends the occasional off-day on the golf course, either playing (to a 12 handicap) or caddying at the local golf club.*

What Got You Where You Are

◆

MIKE GOLIC
WITH ANDREW CHAIKIVSKY

If you want to play, Bob," my father told my oldest brother, who was the first one of us to approach Dad about playing football, "you've got to be ready for all the stuff that's going to happen to you." Lou Golic worked as a bricklayer in Willowick, Ohio. He was a former Marine, with thick forearms and calloused hands. To me, all of five years old, he was the strongest, toughest man in the whole world. He was also my hero.

"If you play football, you're gonna get punched, okay?" he told his wide-eyed eleven-year-old son. "You'll get kicked, scratched up, bitten. You're gonna bleed, and you're gonna break bones."

My brother was floored. Dad had played for a year in college at Indiana and then for several seasons in places like Montreal and Saskatchewan with the Canadian Football League, but all of that had happened in another world, far away from our suburban home in Ohio, long before any of us—Bob, my other brother, Greg, or me—were around. Maybe the game is different now, we thought. Maybe he's trying to scare us. Maybe something awful happened in Canada. Undaunted, we all suited up and took to the practice fields in town, where Dad coached us for St. Mary Magdalene in the CYO league.

Dad was big on fundamentals. Every play begins with the football player in his stance, he told us, and one afternoon after another he'd get us to crouch down to work on nothing but the most basic elements of the perfect, three-point stance. *Toes straight! Get your weight right! Head up!* At home, I'd get down in my stance in front of the mirror in my bedroom and watch myself rise up toward the first instant of contact, again and again, hour after hour. *Thumbs up! Elbows in!* My dad had brought a tackling dummy over and set it up in our tiny backyard, and soon I was coming home from school to hit it a few dozen times, go off to practice, and then return home for more tackling drills. *Drive your feet! Hands inside!* And then, at the end of every long day of bricklaying and coaching, he would make sure to go over my school assignments with me before he went to bed for the night. *The books are just as important, Mike. Work ahead.*

My father was dead right about the brutal realities of the sport, as he was about a lot of things. Along the way, we were punched, scratched up, bitten, and bloodied. But we all went on to play in high school and then college football, all three of us landing at Notre Dame. But when I left home for South Bend and the Fighting Irish, at 18, I didn't leave my father behind. It was his deep voice I heard booming inside my gold helmet on the field during defensive-line drills and in my dorm room as I studied at my desk late into the night. And before every game— whether USC or Michigan State, Pitt or Air Force—I would call him to hear his real voice and ask for his advice. "Never forget what got you where you are, Mike," he told me before my first game. "Remember all the hard work you did. And keep your toes straight, and your elbows in." And for four years, on every Saturday morning during football season, he would remind me to keep my feet moving.

I would later find out that my father had received several offers to play in the NFL but had turned them all down. He was hoping to start a family, and he wanted to be there to help raise his children. So he settled down in a small town on the shores of Lake Erie and found a nine-to-five job that would allow him to spend time with his sons perfecting the three-point stance.

As a kid, needless to say, I couldn't appreciate his sacrifice, and I wouldn't appreciate fully what he had done for his family until I had children of my own.

And I'll admit it, Dad: I've borrowed a lot from you. Flat-out stole it. When my older son, Mike Jr., came to me to ask about playing organized football, I told him, "You'll get kicked, scratched up, bitten. You're gonna bleed, and you're gonna break bones." And when his brother, Jake, one year younger, turned 11, he got the exact same talk. My daughter, Sydney, took up competitive swimming, and she got a lecture too, although I spared her the part about the punches and broken bones. I coached both of my sons through Pop Warner and the youth leagues, working with them on the fundamentals of the stance, blocking, and footwork. There were no tackling dummies in our backyard, but I found a park a few minutes from our home where my sons pushed the SUV across the parking lot, ran, and learned the proper way to catch a football. At night, they'd hit the books and were told to work ahead a little.

When the time came for Mike Jr. to leave for Notre Dame, I was unprepared for how brutal it was to see him go. The day before he left for South Bend, I wanted one more talk with him. He was hanging around the house with friends who had dropped by to wish him good luck in college, when I pulled him aside. "Mike," I said, "I'm going to need about a half hour of your time." We left the house, got in the car, and drove over to the park to our practice field.

As we walked away from the parking lot and toward the trees, I thought back to the times I showed him how to get his hands inside a lineman, the times I saw him hunched over and heaving after wind sprints. I stopped and turned to him. I told my son how proud I was of the man he had become. "Never forget what got you where you are, Mike," I said, almost whispering, "because it will carry you."

And then I hugged him, throwing my weight around his shoulders, and cried.

Mike Golic is co-host of ESPN Radio's Mike & Mike in the Morning *show and an analyst for ESPN's NFL and college football programming. He is a nine-year veteran of the NFL as a defensive tackle, and a former captain of the Notre Dame football team.*

Flip Turn

◆

RON REAGAN

*L*ate summer, 1995. My father and I were lounging, fittingly enough, poolside at my parents' home in Los Angeles. He had recently revealed publicly that he had been diagnosed with Alzheimer's disease, and his powers of recollection had begun to falter—imperceptibly perhaps to strangers but more obviously to those who knew him best. Across formerly clear skies, scraps of mist had begun to drift. Sometimes they were blank patches, sometimes visitors from years past. Familiar names went missing. Different decades tumbled together, producing odd juxtapositions. A couple of minutes earlier, having ventured a few laps, I had climbed out of the pool to join my father under a large umbrella. He had looked me up and down, then suggested, straight-faced, that I try out for the Olympic swim team. I was thirty-seven years old. But in his eyes, who knew? Some memories, though, are remarkably resilient. Old athletes—and I count my father in this category—frequently reach back to long-ago moments of mastery or narrow defeat. I knew where Dad was headed: down a well-worn path, back about twenty-five years to one in a long series of good-natured physical contests we had engaged in as I grew up, back to the moment of my first real triumph, a swimming race both of us had assumed he would win.

"You know what the difference was?"

Rhetorical question. I nodded. I knew.

The race had taken place in our backyard pool in Sacramento the summer I turned twelve. My father had reached the brink of sixty that year, so we were both at an age fraught with danger. I had only just realized that childhood as I had known it was coming to an end; Dad, though I couldn't have appreciated it at the time, must have been hearing the first whispers of mortality.

The pool itself was a rectangle maybe twenty-five yards long—roughly regulation short-course size—rimmed with decorative blue-green tile and coated with fiberglass, which made your skin itch if you spent a lot of time rolling around on the bottom of the deep end reenacting episodes of *Sea Hunt*. There's no telling who challenged whom, but as was our custom, Dad and I lined up in the shallow end on opposite sides of a crescent of steps leading down into the water. My mother was enlisted as a starter's pistol: "On your marks. Get set. Go!"

I had never beaten my father in a swimming race or any athletic contest, as I recall. His philosophy regarding such matters he had made clear a few years before. Once past the age of sentience—seven or so in his reckoning—I would surely know if he was letting me win. This would, in turn, undermine any confidence I might have in a genuine victory achieved at a later date. How much later he never speculated, but I would guess he pictured a strapping college jock finally getting the best of his gray-haired old man. A skinny preadolescent was certainly not part of the plan. As we pushed off for our down-and-back race, I was under no particular pressure to perform, and after a few strokes, upon glancing over to his side of the pool, felt mildly surprised to discover we were dead even.

Now, your average smart-ass twelve-year-old might be undaunted by matching up with a man near hailing distance to a Social Security check, but my father was not your average almost-sixty-year-old. Born before World War I, he grew up long before gyms had sound systems and fancy machines. Weight training was a foreign idea. Yoga would have baffled him. Spandex was out of the question. Real men—men healthily invested in their physical prowess—simply led "vigorous" lives. To that end, Dad rode horses, chopped wood, pounded fence posts, and swam—swam fearlessly in ocean breakers and, at home, back and forth in our pool. These were not casual endeavors squeezed in occasionally between office hours. They occupied a more fundamental, if unforced, place in his life. He had an actor's concern for his appearance and an athlete's pride in the smooth grace of his body's mechanics. At nearly six two and 180 pounds, he was an admirable physical specimen. Though he was older than the other dads I knew by ten, fifteen, even twenty years (he was forty-seven when I was born), I could comfortably assume that he was more than a match for any of them. Gentle by nature, he was nevertheless the kind of man other men instinctively knew to let be. Well into his seventies, after years of relative inactivity behind a desk in the White House, he would retain the power to impress. Brian Mulroney, the former prime minister of Canada, reminiscing recently with my mother, recalled visiting him in the Oval Office. Upon leaving, he remembered, he had clasped my father's arm above the elbow. "My God," he said. "It felt like he was made of iron!"

Down the pool we went. Dad never claimed afterward to have been easing up that first lap, and as far as I could tell, we were both swimming as hard as we could. Incredibly to me, as we approached the end where we would turn and head back, the race was still neck and neck.

A year earlier, as a scrawny eleven-year-old, I had joined the local community swim team and performed without distinction.

I mostly remember the overpowering reek of chlorine, the stinging eyes, and the embarrassing pink paisley Speedos we were
made to wear. I never won a race, partly because I was competing
at the bottom of my age group, but also because the public nature
of the swim meets—crowds of shouting parents, the PA
announcer—threw me. Swimming well requires relaxation.
That's why you always see Olympic swimmers gyrating their
arms and waggling their legs before a race. They're not pumping
up; they're getting loose. Tighten up and you'll enjoy all the
hydrodynamic efficiency of a cinder block. At the only meet my
father attended, I stood on the block, heard my name announced,
and watched a hundred pairs of eyes swivel from Dad to me and
back again as a murmur passed through the crowd. The gun went
off and I hit the water like a bucketful of hammers.

But now I found myself in familiar waters. I had spent the
whole long summer in our pool, practicing somersaults from
the diving board, racing friends up and down, back and forth,
for hours on end, skin gradually wrinkling, till I was called to
dinner. I could swim three lengths of the pool underwater without coming up for air, ignoring the throbbing in my head and
the tightness in my chest until it seemed my lungs would burst.
Now there was no crowd of strangers with an unnatural (to
me) interest in my performance. Just my own mother and
father. And, frustrating as that previous summer's interlude had
been, I had learned a few useful tricks, chief among them the
flip turn.

Most people, when swimming back and forth across a pool will, upon making the far side, reach out with one hand, grab on, and then pull their legs underneath them, the better to push off for the return trip. It's an easy, virtually instinctive action, but terribly inefficient if you're in a hurry. Competitive swimmers, as anyone who follows Olympic swimming events knows, somersault as they reach the wall, allowing them to turn and kick off in one fluid motion.

I had adopted this technique out of necessity and practiced it religiously. And so, as my father and I reached the far end of the pool, I had a secret weapon.

About four feet from the end, I ducked my head and rolled into my turn. This was not yet a foolproof maneuver, but something I could perform reasonably well about seventy-five percent of the time. The odds and perhaps a bit of luck were with me. As I felt both feet plant firmly on the wall, I stole a look in Dad's direction and saw him just reaching for the edge of the pool. Kicking off, I held my body as straight as a nail and arrowed under the water until my momentum began to ebb, then rose to the surface and pulled hard with my right arm, allowing myself a deep drag of air. With my face back in the water, I could see my father complete his turn. I was now a full body length ahead.

Dad could, of course, see me, too. He must have been surprised to find himself falling behind, and I can imagine the tingle of adrenaline as it pulsed through his arms and legs. This could not be happening. Not in a swimming contest.

My father came of age in a river town—Dixon, Illinois. From the ages of fifteen to twenty-one, he worked summers as a lifeguard at the town's beach on the Rock River, Lowell Park. It was a job he was grateful for in those early years of the Depression. An old photograph shows a tall, slim young man, deeply tanned, hair bleached halfway to blond, with long, smooth muscles beneath his singlet. He is not wearing his thick glasses. Extreme nearsightedness had always kept him off the baseball diamond and had limited his utility as a basketball and football player. But nobody sees well underwater. The river was a great equalizer, allowing his natural athletic gifts to find full expression. He was once, he told me, approached by an Olympic scout who invited him to work out with the team preparing for the '32 Games. He turned down the chance to match strokes with Buster Crabbe because he couldn't afford to pass up his summer pay. As far as I know, he still holds the record for swimming from the park to the river's far bank and back. During those seven summers, he saved seventy-seven people from drowning, marking each victory over the deceptively swift current by carving a notch on a beached log. He was a small-town hero. Water was his element.

It was not all suntans and hooking up behind the changing stalls, this lifeguarding job. Rivers are dangerous. Mix in people determined to drown themselves and the dangers increase exponentially. I'd heard the stories, often couched as lessons. A river may look placid and smooth on its surface as it meanders slowly between its banks, but beneath the skin it hides whirls and undertows, powerful currents that will sap the strength of the strongest swimmer. Water was, my father stressed, an element to be respected. He had learned early that the shortest route from bank to bank was never a straight line but a swooping upstream arc. Work with water, he advised all his children, never against it; water will always be stronger than you are.

People posed a different challenge. Women, he recalled, were always grateful to be rescued, and some, he knew, would deliberately stray too far toward the middle of the river for the opportunity to be rescued by him. Men, on the other hand, would generally offer thanks only at the urging of their girl-friends, and even then grudgingly. Would've been fine. Not really in trouble, but thanks anyway. As he told it, Dad would never really acknowledge these dissemblings but just nod and keep whittling a fresh notch in his log.

Toward the end of summer, brawny farm boys finished with the harvest would begin arriving at the park. Most rarely encountered water deeper than an irrigation ditch and would invariably underestimate the river's power. In the grip of the current, exhausted, they would go vertical and begin to struggle. Their frantic clawing would on occasion need to be subdued with a right cross to the jaw in order to effect a safe rescue. Then there was the blind man. He was a towering hulk of a fellow, and Dad had spotted him the moment he entered the park. How, he wondered, would he ever manage to pull such a man to safety once he started fighting for his life? Sure enough, away from the beach the man paddled and within minutes was swept into the middle of the river. A noise went up from the assembled bathers as his big arms began slapping ineffectually at the surface, but my father was already in the water. Swimming out, following the bobbing head downstream, he wondered whether this might be his last rescue attempt. Drowning people will literally grasp at straws, anything for a last breath of air. Sightless, confused, and fearing for his life, this man would lock the first thing that came to hand in a death grip. That first thing would be his rescuer. Dad imagined them in a grotesque embrace, rolling along the river bottom toward the next town downstream. But to his immense relief, when he finally reached the man and put a hand on his shoulder, the reaction was immediate and total compliance. Accustomed his whole life to being led by others, he associated human touch with safety and instantly relaxed.

Ten yards out and the white blur at my father's heels told me he was kicking furiously. But despite an early surge, he had not closed the gap. I felt a rush of pure exhilaration: I was going to win! You have to swim slow to swim fast. This is not the answer to a Zen koan, merely one of the paradoxes involved in propelling yourself through an alien medium. In past years, other races, I might have shortened my stroke, chopping at the water in an effort to reach the finish a bit quicker—a beginner's mistake. Now I did the opposite, reaching farther, pulling longer, and as a result sped up. Five yards; three feet; touch. Raising my head out of the water, I looked over just in time to see my father glide to the wall.

My mother had been standing at the side of the pool since we set off, rehearsing in her mind, I suppose, the little speech she would give me to soothe the sting of defeat: You nearly did it; you've really improved; maybe next year. Now, sucking air through a victorious grin, I looked at her face and saw something new, an expression I didn't recognize. There was happiness on my behalf, no doubt, but mixed with something else, something very much like sadness. She turned to my father, and he saw it, too. He didn't have to ask.

"Huh. Well, whattaya know?" When he looked in my direction, I was still wearing my thrill-of-victory smile. "Congratulations," he said. "That was a good swim."

Fathers and sons have been competing since before dirt and, I imagine, have always experienced the same conflicted emotions. There is little to add to this oedipal saga; it's an ancient story. For sons, there is the thrill of holding your own in the world of men. But the price paid is a heavy one. To claim your prize, you must vanquish the god of your childhood. The strongest man on earth, the dad who can whip all other dads, must be brought down, made ordinary and all too human. Fathers, however proud of their progeny's success, recognize this defeat as a small death, a painful step down a road with a certain end. My mother surely felt this, and as I returned to thrashing around in the deep end and my father climbed slowly out of the pool, I saw her approach with a towel and place it tenderly over his shoulders.

It wasn't till later that evening that the question arose: "Did you do one of those flip turns?"

Summer was nearly over. Through some sort of unspoken understanding, neither Dad nor I requested a rematch. Soon the weather would turn chill and I would be back in school. By the following summer, one year older and that much stronger, I would be out of reach. My father and I never raced again.

And that was nearly that. But four years later, there would be one final struggle, an epic arm-wrestling match fought to a stalemate on the coral-colored shag of my parents' dressing room. My mother was reduced to the role of nervous spectator—there was no need for an official start, just a quick, synchronized one-two-three-go. In years past, these matches had followed a set routine: Dad would allow me to slowly push his arm over nearly horizontal, then recover to the vertical, where I would struggle to exhaustion before he gently vanquished me. This time, nobody was faking it.

Naturally, my father had an arm-wrestling story. A few years earlier, as governor, he had traveled to Petaluma, California, for the World Arm-Wrestling Championships. A photographer had posed him with one of the contenders as if they were competing. In the interest of realism—or perhaps out of sheer perversity—he then suggested they "y'know, go at it a little." Dad may have been overly enthusiastic. The following day, his office got a call from the competition. My father had broken the man's arm.

We would battle for several long minutes, faces inches apart, neither of us able to budge the other, till veins bulged and sweat ran into our eyes. I think we were both stunned at how ferociously we were fighting just to keep from being outdone. By this time, my mother had seen enough. "Stop it! Stop it!" The anxiety in her voice brought both of us up short. We agreed to call it a draw, and that was that. I can still see us sprawled on the rug, panting, in the afterglow of combat. Dad's face had a slightly surprised look. Truthfully, I felt a bit ashamed. I was old enough by then to grasp that continuing to push and challenge would verge on cruelty. There was no longer any point. It was over.

In years to come, neither my father nor I ever referred to our arm-wrestling match. It may as well not have happened. Our earlier swimming race, however, attained an honored place in family lore. Again and again, the story would bubble up in conversation, usually at Dad's instigation. My victory was always gracefully acknowledged, and I always responded that I'd had a great teacher. But the flip turn, as it transpired, had become a useful, face-saving asterisk for Dad. Yes, I'd won, but by employing a technique not practiced in his day. Were it not for that . . . who knows?

That my father should have recalled our race with such clarity no longer surprises me. The unimaginable so easily becomes the unforgettable. Seemingly ageless, accustomed to prevailing over time and nature, Dad did not yet feel old enough that long-ago afternoon to be beaten up and down the pool by a son who was still too young. Over the years, my father and I had raced each other countless times; all but one run together in a blur. His loss, so unexpected for both of us, sealed our memory.

Late summer, 1995. Another pool. My father and I sat beneath the shade of our umbrella, squinting out into the afternoon light. Alzheimer's will have its inexorable way, and Dad seldom swam anymore. Now there was mostly the past, some of it fading, some not.

"It was your flip turn that did it. Till then, you know, we were even."

Watching the sun beat down on the water, casting its net of light over the bottom of the pool, I didn't bother to turn in his direction.

"Yes, we were even."

Ron Reagan is a contributor to MSNBC. He is often seen on Hardball *with Chris Matthews. Since his father's death from Alzheimer's in 2004, Reagan has been speaking out on the subject of stem cell research, and advocating for increased research and federal funding. He is an active member of the Creative Coalition, a first amendment rights group. As a special correspondent for* Good Morning America, *Reagan interviewed entertainment icons ranging from Elizabeth Taylor to Mikhail Baryshnikov. He has contributed to* Newsweek, The New Yorker, Playboy, *the* Los Angeles Times, Esquire, *and* Interview.

My Dad, the Bookie

◆

MICHAEL J. AGOVINO

I t was Super Bowl Sunday, the only day of the year my mother served dinner in front of the television set. She knew that my father had a vested financial interest in the game and that I was a boy who cared deeply about sports. So she conceded: dinner in the living room, in front of the Trinitron. I suspect she enjoyed it.

The menu was a concession, too, solely for me this time. Gone was our usual midwinter Southern Italian Sunday feast: a homemade *ragu* over rigatoni, with braciola, sausage, broccoli rabe on the side and a carafe of Valpolicella. No, on this day, my mother, ever so desperate to put meat on my little bones, served up my favorite: roast beef, potatoes, Boston lettuce and mountains of green beans sautéd with garlic and olive oil.

My older sister refused to take part. She always hated two things—red meat and sports. Above all, she hated my father's gambling, the ebb and flow of anxiety that came with it, the screaming matches it provoked between my parents, the dark silences after a bad day at "the office," the absurdity of risking our future on Tampa Bay or TCU or some horse, maybe Foolish Pleasure.

For my father, gambling and bookmaking was a second job, his clandestine second life. He had been gambling in some form or another since FDR's second term. By the 1980s, it had become his main source of income.

On that Super Bowl Sunday in 1984, in our Bronx apartment, twenty-two stories above the rickety treetops, the three of us—my parents and I—watched the Washington Redskins play the Los Angeles Raiders. The Redskins were the defending title-holders and a three-point favorite. My father wagered heavily on the Raiders. How heavily, I don't know; I knew not to ask.

He never had favorite teams—gamblers and bookmakers can't get attached, can't afford to—but he had a thing for the Raiders. Kenny Stabler might have started it; my father had a predilection for lefties. And the Raiders were always the bad guys. That helped.

Washington had the self-aggrandizing quarterback Joe Theismann and the impudent receiving corps known as the Smurfs. The Raiders had the stoic Tom Flores and the unfashionable Jim Plunkett—two scions of industrious Chicano laborers who came up the hard way.

In the third quarter, when the game was still a game, there was a play—a very famous play. Perhaps you remember it. Marcus Allen, bright, young, stealthy, took a handoff from Plunkett. He ran left to the line of scrimmage, saw it was clogged, "stopped on a dime," spun 180 degrees to the right, got a feeble but well-intentioned block from the creaky-limbed Plunkett and turned upfield. For a few interminable seconds, we didn't talk, we didn't chew, we didn't breathe. Our eyes widened, and we watched Marcus Allen run. He kept on running, a silver streak, away from the pack for some seventy yards and a touchdown. Roasted potatoes flew into the air, and green beans, and shouts of joy. My sister, eavesdropping, came out of her room, relieved. For now it was apparent the Raiders would win. Her perpetually overdue tuition at Clark University would be paid. Outside, the Bronx resonated with horns and howls, at least our multiracial, multiethnic, occasionally tensioned corner of the Bronx, an eyesore of gray schematic towers called Co-op City. Marcus Allen saved the world that night.

This is what it was like to live with a bookmaker. When my father won, we saw things. Doors opened, views expanded. He liked to think of himself as a capitalist hero. He would tell us over dinner that he "made the wheels turn." For him, money was something you enjoyed. It went to things like books, food, wine, delicacies, opera tickets, music lessons, and trips to museums—in Delft.

How much did my father win? There was never a final tally, not that Sunday nor any other. As in any business, he had a gross and a net, the difference being how much he owed. When he didn't win, when things hit rock bottom, bills would not be paid. The fee for his gallbladder surgery at New York Hospital in 1977 wasn't settled until the early '90s. He'd go six months without paying the phone bill and the telephone company would shut off our service or at least prevent us from making outgoing calls. "God forbid of an emergency," my mother would say.

To buy time, my father raised the already fine art of check bouncing to something metaphysical. Eventually, people wouldn't accept anything but cash from him. He probably averted trouble, narrowly, a dozen times, maybe more. What kind of trouble, I'm not sure. I know he borrowed from people, maybe bad people, borrowed from one to pay another.

When I worked up the gumption, and as I child I wasn't blessed with gumption, I'd ask how much he'd won or lost and he'd simply say, "Don't worry" or "Worry about your school-work." By the time I was in college, I was more aggressive in my questioning, especially when I'd meet him on a corner near the NYU campus in the final hour of late registration, two weeks into the semester, and he'd be in a cold, panicked sweat, bank check in hand, with me thinking he'd have a stroke between Greene and Mercer. He was fifty-eight then, no longer permitted to have a credit card. I was eighteen, a freshman in college, making four-something an hour at the NYU bookstore, and I had my choice of Visa, Mastercard or Discover. He wouldn't answer. He would just turn reticent.

My mother tried to save. She would stash what she could in her James Beard cookbook so he couldn't get to it, squander it on the early daily double. She made my sister and me swear not to tell him where the money was. Not that there was much: a few fives, tens and twenties. Just enough to pay the pharmacist and maybe a taxi driver if sickly me needed to see Dr. Printz on Burke Avenue. When my mother knew my father was short on cash—that is, when he came to me or my sister for change to buy subway tokens—she began to worry. As far as I know, he never did try to uncover her cache, not unless he searched the house at night, when we were all asleep. He never could sleep very well.

Other people, most others we knew, had assets—houses, cars, savings or retirement accounts: "security," as my mother would say. Even my father's "customers"—that's what he called them—had plenty put away. Mostly Wall Street types, Jews, Italians, Irish, the odd WASP, they gambled simply for sport. One of them, my mother reminded us, had a Swiss bank account. A Swiss bank account!" My father borrowed from his pension and his IRA.

"It's not normal," she'd say loudly, decrying our lifestyle.

"I know it's not normal," he'd say.

Sure it was odd, but it was all we knew. My sister and I couldn't have friends over between six and eight at night, between noon and two on weekends. Our phones—we had two extensions, one private, one for the customers—would ring off the hook. It would look suspicious to visitors.

Not that our neighbors could afford to pass judgment. Co-op City had a cast of 55,000 oddball characters. Who drank, who smacked around his wife, who was a degenerate horseplayer, who was a petty gossip, who never should have been a parent, who scrawled graffiti in the stairwells, who pissed in the elevators, who was a corrupt cop or a junkie-to-be—this was common knowledge in Co-op City. We had no Main Street or Pine Street or Fourth of July parade. Just cherry bombs in garbage cans. But my family seemed odd to the oddballs. We were the freaks. Jetting off one day, finding eviction notices on the door the next. Steven, half-Italian, half-Jewish, would ask me in third grade, "Is your father in the Mafia?" The kids, even teachers, would look at me and wait for a response. They didn't know what to think when we went round the room, reporting on summer vacations. Everyone else said Lake George or Shorehaven. I said Lisbon or Rabat or Amsterdam. My teachers thought what Steven thought. They had the same mentality as a third grader.

But Steven was wrong. We weren't connected. And we certainly didn't look like we were. My mother was taken for an elementary-school teacher. Old Jewish women would say to her on Friday afternoon, "Shabbat shalom." People mistook my father for my grandfather. He looked as conformist as they come, bifocaled, in conservative matte blazers, no jewelry, a balding head, hair mostly gray. And he was terribly hard of hearing—except when the phone rang. Sometimes he'd run to the receiver, pick it up and discover nothing but a dial tone. Often the phone hadn't even been ringing.

My father had a full-time job—quotidian bureaucratic work for the city's Department of Welfare. He hated it, for thirty-five years. It was there, at his day job, that he struck up friendships with the playwright Loften Mitchell and with the artist Romare Bearden, who was a caseworker. Getting to know these men was a bright spot, one of the few, in my father's workday.

That was in the late '50s, early '60s, when our country was less educated but smarter somehow, more engaged. My father and Bearden would talk about Coleman Hawkins and Johnny Hodges, Vermeer and Giotto, the Rock and Clay. One day the humble Bearden said, "Hey, come to my studio; I make these collages." He offered to make one for my father. Not wanting to seem presumptuous (*scustumad*, in the Neapolitan dialect of my father's birthplace, East Harlem), my father said, "No, no, really, I couldn't."

"What that would be worth today," my mother would say for years afterward. Then my father would say it again: "What that would be worth today." When I was much older, I went to the Harlem home of author Albert Murray. There, in the bathroom, was a very small work of Bearden's. It was exquisite, teeming with humanity and language, so much happening in so small a space. It was the kind of collage I now imagine Bearden would have given my father. As I stood in Murray's bathroom, I thought, Why couldn't we have one of those, something of rare beauty and value?

Of course, my father might have sold our Bearden in a fit of financial desperation. Then again, I have to remind myself that art was sacred to him, that Bearden was much closer to Albert Murray than he was to my father. Murray had fourteen original Beardens, large and small, around his apartment. Still, there is a photograph that exists somewhere of my father and Bearden taken after my father was one of a handful of people who spoke at a farewell party for Bearden when Bearden left the department to devote himself to his art, and I can't help but think that one day, a special day or a sad day, that photograph and a transcendent little Bearden collage will be brought to me. I know in reality this will never happen. My father's story is true: He didn't want to be presumptuous. His collage exists only in Albert Murray's bathroom or in a gallery on 57th Street between Madison and Park.

Unlike Bearden, my father stuck it out at the Department of Welfare. He had no viable alternative—it was the best he could do with a high school education. Stuyvesant High School, but still high school. After the service, after the war, Colgate University was an option, but he didn't go that way. Joining the Genovese crime family was another option. Frank Costello was the man in charge in East Harlem, and he was looking to recruit bright kids from the neighborhood. My father had a willing and able sponsor, but he didn't go that way, either.

My father had a talent for something; for what, I've never been sure. It was something intangible, something suited to his strengths; the inherent disposition of a gambler, mettle, nerve, out-and-out gall. I wish I had some of these things, more guts, more guile, a romantic sense of risk, equanimity, smarts. Instead I have the college degree he never got.

When the two of us ended up alone, at a ball game or walking around the city (never camping, never golfing), he would talk to me—his nine-year-old—man to man. He didn't want to put me on the spot, but he couldn't help himself. By rationalizing to his son, he rationalized to himself: "Your mother doesn't understand" ... "My job can barely put food on the table" ... "It's a business; please understand," I would nod plaintively, by now the ballgame or whatever outing we had planned was ruined.

He had to do whatever he did. For whatever reasons, however opaque, he didn't go to college. Instead, he split his time between the Garden and the Met, read books, gambled, did some bookmaking. He also did tax returns, first for a professional outfit, then mainly for friends and their friends. He worked cheap; word got around. He just hinted at a figure—something below reasonable—and often got in return only a bottle of hard liquor, which he never drank.

He wasn't alone in his odd, elliptical sort of defiance, his hostility. A lot of the East Harlem recalcitrants he grew up with tried to tweak the system and give scapegoat society a collective fuck you, from Pleasant Avenue to the world. Some played it safe, bought two-family houses in the Bronx or Queens, but others grew bitter, self-destructed or vanished off the face of the earth. We heard stories, the same ones again and again, from my father, of Bense. I don't even know his real name. He was an East Harlem boy, my father's best friend, and all I remember from those stories is how he choked a dog to death because it barked at him the wrong way. Bense was one of those who fell off the earth, but I can't recall how. My father said he was a great friend; fiercely loyal, free with a buck, would challenge guys twice his size to protect his friends. My mother just talked about his disconcerting gaze. She did everything she could to keep us away from the Benses of the world.

My father couldn't work for anyone; that was another of his defining traits. He was a Manhattanite, but he was never invited to its upper precincts. He'd see art (Mantegna, Velázquez and Rubens were his Ruth, Gehrig and DiMaggio), see the latest Kurosawa or Fellini, read the Greek tragedies or Seneca the Stoic, or venture up to the decaying Polo Grounds to "lay a few dollars" on Warren Spahn when the Milwaukee Braves played the Giants. Spahn was his boy. Later Ron Guidry, good Cajun, was his talisman. Nolan Ryan, as my mother never let us forget, brought nothing but dread.

Most Sunday afternoons in autumn and winter, some of the biggest gambling days of the year, my sister would lock herself in her room, listen to Blondie records, and immerse herself in homework, obsessed with good grades. I didn't study as much, just enough to get by, and for the most part I didn't mind my father's second job. Only when we went to a game and he needed the other team to win would it dampen my mood. Imagine rooting for the Kansas City Kings against the Knicks, the San Diego Padres against the Mets, because you fear your father might get hurt if the visiting team doesn't cover. When you're a boy, your father is still more important to you than Louis Orr or Dave Kingman.

In later years, I resented him and admired him. I learned to see things. He taught me how to improvise. And we had Tommy Hearns. Sugar Ray Leonard versus Tommy Hearns, September 1981. We went to Madison Square Garden for the closed-circuit telecast. My father met me at 23rd and Broadway; there was a bus from the Bronx that let out there. We took a short walk to Paul & Jimmy's on Irving Place for dinner. Then he took this little seventh grader, the envy of I.S. 181 that day, to the fight with a New York crowd, 20,000, no kids, all grown-ups, all men, some scary. In the thirteenth round, when a desperate, puffy-eyed Leonard, behind on points, threw a last-ditch roundhouse right and Hearns's spindly legs buckled, we yelled together, "Stay up, Tommy." Tommy went down—three times—and one round later the ref stopped the fight. We rushed out onto Seventh Avenue, rancid and teeming.

My mother worried. She thought I would grow up to be a gambler, I would casually ask at the dinner table. "Daddy, what's a parlay? What's a two-team teaser? How much is a nickel? How much is a dime? What's a wheel bet? What's the line on the Vikings game this week? . . . *Three and a half,* that's it?"

"See what you're teaching him?" she'd say.

He would send me to the candy store to get *The New York Times*, the *Post* and a touting sheet called *The Sports Eye* before I could even reach the countertop. Some of the old men—two dollar bettors whom my father looked down on—thought it was cute. Who knows what else they thought?

We never owned a house, had virtually no savings, and barely owned a car—you couldn't really count the used-up gray-and-black 1960-something Buick LeSabre that was stolen twice, both times when we were in New Orleans. But we saw places: Italy in '73; Spain, Portugal and Morocco in '76; England and Holland in '79; Martinique in '80; St Martin in '81; the Dominican Republic in '82; Mexico, Canada and Charleston. South Carolina, in '83; Switzerland in '85, Six times we went to Puerto Rico, where my father had two gambling friends, a Romanian and a half-Pole, half-Puerto Rican, who would pare down their debt by letting us stay in their Santurce apartments.

One night in the early spring of 1984, with those Super Bowl winnings still trickling in, my parents talked about the summer. The Bronx would be unforgiving in July, they reasoned; France would be nice. (At last they agreed on something.) Two months later, we were bound for Orly Airport. Off to Paris, Chartres, the Loire Valley, then Versailles for an afternoon, across to Strasbourg, down to Lyon, then to Nice, where the people looked like us, tiptoeing around dog shit in Aix-en-Provence, west into Languedoc, to Carcassonne in the foothills of the Pyrenees. "On a clear day," a man said to a child, "you can see Spain if you squint." We went way up north, fourteen hours by overnight train, to Rouen, the bane of Joan of Arc, before returning to a Paris, bright and perfect.

It was a special trip. My sister and I were getting older; more and more of those tuition bills dotted the horizon. My father's losses were mounting. Already, U.S. marshals had rung the bell to remind us we owed four months' rent, handing my mother the eviction notice.

We managed Geneva the following year, unexpectedly, thanks maybe to Villanova. But in 1984, we figured France to be our last trip together, though none of us said so. We talked about staying in Paris, for a week, a month, forever. It was comforting. Eight francs to the dollar. We met only one haughty Frenchman the entire month. But we had to get back, back to reality, back to our waiting, anomalous Bronx. A new football season was about to start. Doors would open or close with each Monday-morning line. On Sunday nights, I would peek into my father's bedroom, sometimes pitch-black, after his screeching big-band tapes were through, Benny Goodman and Basie and Jimmy Lunceford, and see him staring straight ahead, sometimes muttering softly the line: Cincy minus seven, Denver plus two and a half, Texas Tech pick 'em. Now, when the sun is just right, at such an angle where you have to use your hand as a visor, and the air has the warmth of July in it, numbers like that can carry me back to southwestern France, standing on a dusty bluff in Carcassonne. If you squint hard enough, on the clearest of days, you can see Spain.

Michael J. Agovino has been an editor at Esquire *and* Newsweek. *His writing has appeared in those publications as well as in* The New York Times, GQ, *the* New York Observer, Slate, Salon, Elle, *and many others. His memoir* The Bookmaker *will be published by HarperCollins. He was born and raised in New York City.*

Holy Ground

◆

WRIGHT THOMPSON

AUGUSTA, Georgia—Most everything makes me think about my daddy, and this morning, of all the stupid reasons to fight back tears in public, it's chipped beef on toast. I'm sitting at the corner table on the clubhouse veranda, waiting for Arnold Palmer to hit the ceremonial first shot of the Masters. Man, my father loved watching Arnie. To do it from the veranda with a plate of chipped beef? Hotty Toddy, brother. Only, the excitement of incredible moments like this is muted for me now. I've learned in the past three years that I did many things solely to tell Daddy about them later.

The crowd stands on Washington Road, waiting for the gates to open. For a moment, the course is quiet. Birds chirp. Mowers drone. Soon, another lucky diner asks if he can join me. His food arrives first. As we talk a bit, bundled against the chill, he looks at the empty space in front of me.

"What did you order?" he asks.

"Chipped beef on toast," I say. He laughs.

"Breakfast of champions," he says.

"It was my dad's favorite meal," I explain.

"Did you ever bring him here?" he asks.

There is a silence. "No," I say, turning away.

Daddy watched the Masters every year. He dreamed of attending just one, and he's always on my mind when I come here for my job. Indeed, for all of us lucky enough to actually walk through these gates, we cannot leave without having thoughts of our daddies, for Augusta National is a place for fathers and sons. Davis Love III navigates the same fairways as Davis Love Jr. New fathers carefully hold toddler hands. "Can you see?" you'll hear them say. Strong arms tenderly steer stooped backs. "Look out, Dad," you'll hear them say softly. That is Augusta.

When Jack Nicklaus finished his final round ever at the Masters, his eyes welled on the green. He glanced at his son, who was caddying for him, and repeated his own father's last words, "Don't think it ain't been charming." As Jack ended his relationship with this special place, he looked at his son and thought of his father. That is Augusta.

When Tiger Woods won for the first time, his eyes searched the gallery near the scoring shed for Earl Woods. They hugged, Tiger's head cradled on his father's shoulder. And when he walked off the green almost a decade later, and Earl Woods was no longer there, Tiger remembered that shoulder and he mourned. That is Augusta.

This, too, is Augusta: me, needing a daddy more than ever, finishing the chipped beef on toast, walking the grounds in search of fatherly wisdom. Me, a thirty-year-old man, who failed in my promise to bring Daddy to this place he longed to visit, unable to control my emotions when I see a father and a son standing by the first fairway. The boy is a half-head taller and growing. Both wear blue Penn State gear. I see myself in that boy, standing with his father, both thinking they have all the time in the world.

◆　◆　◆

We were a father and son in my dad's imagination before my parents even knew I was a boy. On the day I was born, he sat down and wrote a letter to himself, cataloging his thoughts as his first child came into the world. He called me his son, with daughter written each time in parentheses, just in case. When I arrived, before my mother even cleared her head, he had already filled out the birth certificate. There was never even a discussion of what I would be called. "Walter Wright Thompson, Jr.," he wrote.

Walter Wright Thompson, Sr. had grown up in the Mississippi sticks with three brothers. Many of the traits my friends would recognize in me came from him. He loved to be the loudest guy in the room, and he loved telling stories, and hearing them, too. He loved his favorite places to eat beyond any normalcy and the sound of the ocean and the hum of late-night conversation. He loved working hard.

His own dad was a tough man with unfulfilled boyhood dreams. Nothing was good enough. When my daddy, a star quarterback, would run for three touchdowns and throw for two more, Big Frazier would be waiting after to ask why he'd missed that tackle early in the third quarter. Daddy decided that when he had a son of his own, he'd do it differently. He'd give his whole heart, shower all the love and attention and approval he could muster. He would be a good daddy. A sweet daddy.

I remember tailgating before Ole Miss football games, him throwing passes just far enough away that I'd have to dive. I remember Destin, Florida, when I dropped my favorite stuffed animal, Sweetie, and didn't tell him until we got back to the condo. He spent hours looking for that rabbit, and he found it, too. I keep it around, but I don't ever tell anyone why. When I look at it, I can feel how much he loved me. I remember skipping school to go fishing, and I remember promising not to tell Mama. I remember him always reminding me that "you catch more flies with honey than with vinegar" and "if it feels wrong, it is." I remember him taking me to see *Superman III* the night it opened, even though I was in trouble; I remember watching *The Guns of Navarone* a thousand times with him. And I remember, as clear as if it happened yesterday, that April day in 1986 when Jack Nicklaus charged toward his sixth green jacket.

I was playing in the other room, probably with that G.I. Joe aircraft carrier, when he called my name. I didn't want to go. He called again. So I went into their bedroom. He was lying on his stomach.

"Jack Nicklaus is going to win the Masters, son, and you've got to watch this. You will remember this for the rest of your life."

So we lay there, my feet only coming to his knees, watching. I was ten. He was forty, six years younger than Jack, and he cried when the final putt went in. I can't remember now if I'd ever seen him cry before.

The years slipped away, but every April, we lay down on our stomachs—tumbuckets, he called 'em—and oohed over the azaleas and aahed over Amen Corner. Each time, he'd smile and mention that, one day, he'd sure like to see what such a place must look like in person. He grew older. I went to college and, as a freshman, called him to ask if he was watching this kid named Tiger Woods. He was. I sat in the Phi Delta Theta house three states away. I could picture him lying on his stomach.

Home didn't feel so far away.

◆ ◆ ◆

It has been ten years. I no longer watch the Masters on television, and I pinch myself each time I get the credential, though

I try to hide it. Sportswriters are supposed to act jaded, right? I'm sitting right now with colleagues in the press center interview room. Tiger Woods is at the dais, no longer the kid he was a decade ago, either. Normally, he's full of boring blather, using a lot of words but carefully saying nothing. Only now he's talking about fathers and sons, about losing one and gaining another. I lean in a bit. He talks about regret, and the things he wishes he'd done. He talks about what kind of parent he'd like to be.

"Here I am, thirty-one years old," he says, "and my father is getting smarter every year. It's just amazing. But hopefully, my child, down the road a little bit, will say the same thing."

That, to me, is the definition of growing up. There comes a time when every son starts the slow transition to father. Mine began four years ago. My dad felt pain and went to the doctor. A scan revealed cancer. He was fifty-seven years old, with marriages to attend and grandkids to spoil. Instead? He was in a fight for his life. He pulled into a parking lot on the way home and read the report. It said something about the pancreas. He understood he was in trouble. Up a creek without a paddle in a screen-bottomed boat, he'd say.

But the man had never backed down. Once, in college, he knocked out an All-SEC football player for messing with his brother. He attacked this disease just as viciously. After the first chemo session, he stopped at a greasy fast-food chain to get a sack of sliders, an f-you to the poison. To walk through a hospital with him was to understand his gift for life. All the nurses and doctors and patients—especially the patients who sat through the treatments alone—called him by name. For each, he had a kind word and a smile. He raised the energy level of every room he entered.

We took a fishing trip he'd always wanted to take. I knew there wasn't any time to waste. We spent a glorious few days on a river in Arkansas, filling our cooler with trout, talking late into the night. "I'm not afraid," he told me. Before leaving the fishing camp, I made a reservation for a year later. This, he said, we had to do again. "We'll be here," he said, almost whispering. "I guarantee it."

Back home, he spent hours alone, at his spot behind the house. There was a canebreak out there, and a brick wall, and tall oak trees and a creek. He'd sit there, long past sunset, and he'd think about his life. It's where he prepared to die. Once, my mom pointed out toward his silhouette, tears filling her eyes and running down her cheeks, and said, "It just breaks my heart. I think he's scared."

Still, he read the right books, by preachers and by Lance Armstrong, and he'd make damn clear he didn't want to know the odds. So we didn't tell. But we knew. And they weren't good. I wept the first time I Googled pancreatic cancer. What would I do without a daddy?

Only, sometimes, it does happen like in the movies. He responded to the chemo. The doctors saw the tumors shrinking and, finally, a scan revealed he was cancer free. We couldn't believe it. He didn't act surprised.

Of course, I was at the Masters when we got the news.

Daddy and I made immediate plans for a vacation. We'd go back to Destin, where he'd found my stuffed animal. I bought the tickets and, the day after the tournament, I drove to Atlanta, met him at the airport and, together, we flew south. In the air, I gave him my Masters media credential. He collected them, kept them hanging by his bathroom mirror to remind himself that his son had gone places. He treasured the parking passes, too, and, faithfully affixed them to his truck after I left Augusta.

In Florida, we sat in lounge chairs by the ocean. We ate quail and grits, and Daddy talked the place into giving us the recipe. We drove in a Mustang convertible with the top rolled back, and we made plans. His reprieve made him realize that he needed to stop practicing law sixteen hours a day and do those things he'd always dreamed of doing. He wanted to visit China, stand above those gorges. He wanted to see Tuscany, rent a villa.

Mostly, he wanted to go with me to the Masters.

"It's a done deal," I told him. "Done deal."

We celebrated his birthday. I picked up dinner, the first and only time I ever did that. We laughed, and I gave him a present: a black Masters windbreaker. He held it up before him, glanced at me, words failing. He slipped it on and went outside to read. I shuffled off to bed. With the cancer gone, time was no longer precious; we had all the time in the world. But something made me take one last look, seeing him sitting on the balcony, thin and pale, the waves crashing somewhere out in the blackness, a thin ribbon of smoke rising from an ashtray.

◆   ◆   ◆

Three months later, I got the call. I was in Pittsburgh for a Chelsea-AC Roma soccer game. Mama was crying. They'd run some tests and the results were in.

"It's cancer," she sobbed.

Two months later, he felt bad and went to the hospital. The doctors weren't too worried. Mama and Daddy asked, "Do we need to call the boys?" Love is a strange thing—you go from a fraternity dance to the altar of a church to a cold hospital room, asking: Is one of us about to die? The doctors said no.

They were wrong.

As I sat in Kansas City, watching the movie *Miracle*, my father passed away. It was only a few days away from our return fishing trip. My mom didn't want to tell me until I got back to Mississippi, so she made what had to be the toughest phone call of her life. After watching her husband of thirty-four years take his final breath, she called me and said it didn't look good and that I needed to bring a suit. I refused to pack funeral clothes, holding out hope.

The next morning, I landed in Memphis and took the escalator down to the baggage claim. I saw my brother, William, at the bottom. I smiled and waved. He just shook his head. At that moment, my mother stepped out from behind a sign. I knew.

"Your sweet daddy died," she said.

I dropped my suitcase and cell phone. Someone got them, I guess. The next moments are fragments. A parking garage, a silent car, relatives, pats, looks away, driving, buildings, thirst, I'm really thirsty, could someone please get me some damn water, traffic, interstate on-ramp, off-ramp, driving. I could only get out one question.

"Was he scared?" I asked.

Mama shook her head no.

The funeral week was a blur. When we picked out his favorite Zegna sport coat, I went into his bathroom, holding those Masters credentials in my hands. I took them out, slipping them into the jacket pocket. If there was an Augusta National in heaven, I wanted him to get in.

"I'm sorry, Daddy," I said to the air, "you didn't get to go."

Seven months later, I was back at Augusta. It was a hard week. I wore a pair of his shoes around the course, trying to walk it for him. I wrote a column about it for my newspaper and, as I'm doing now, tried to find some closure. Then, I believed my grief ended with the catharsis of the last paragraph. I was naive, as I found when I returned to Augusta in the coming years, finding my pain stronger each time.

Exactly a year after he died, my family gathered at home. We had a baby tree, grown from an acorn that came from the sturdy oaks in Ole Miss' legendary Grove, where Daddy spent so many happy afternoons. We gathered at the spot where he'd sat, where he'd made his peace, and we dug a small hole, filling it in with the roots of the sapling and potting soil. I carefully patted down the earth around the stalk. Then it was done.

That night, I couldn't sleep. Outside, rain poured down, soaking the tender roots. It rained an inch, then two, then more. The creek rose. I worried about my daddy's tree, so I went to stand guard. Soaked, cold, shivering, I stood by the tree, protecting it as I'd been unable to protect him.

I stared out past the canebreak and the brick wall and the creek. The sky was black. I wondered if Daddy was looking down on me, watching me, seeing my successes and failures. I wondered if he was proud of me. I wondered if there was a way I could still ask questions and he could still give me answers. I'd always counted on him for the answers.

"Daddy," I said aloud, "are you out there?"

I waited, but I heard no answer, just the shattering windows of water falling from the sky.

◆ ◆ ◆

Maybe I'll find those answers out here, at this place he loved so much. Is that crazy? Nothing seems crazy to me anymore. The grass shines like polished green mirrors. The flowers explode with a rainbow of shrapnel: pinks, purples, whites, yellows. Mostly, though, I see the fathers and sons, like the Livelys from Charleston, West Virginia, sitting in front of me, watching the par-three tournament. For fifteen years, he'd entered the lottery for practice-round tickets. This year, he won, and he took his two sons out of school for a day. I wanted that to be us.

Down by Ike's Pond, television reporter Jim Gray interviews players as they leave the course. He asks what I'm working on, and when I tell him, he nods, pointing to a white-haired man sitting in the sun by the water. It's Jerry Gray, his father, and for sixteen years, he's come with his famous son to Augusta. "It's the only week we spend together all year," Jim tells me, and, again, I'm jealous. It doesn't seem fair. Sometimes, a boy needs a daddy.

I just got married about a year ago, and I knew he'd have loved to stand up at the front of that church. In a way, he was: In the pocket of my tuxedo, I carried his yellow LIVESTRONG bracelet and, as Sonia started down the aisle, I rubbed it once, just to let him know, if he was watching, that he might be gone but he wasn't forgotten.

I just bought my first house, and I knew he'd know whether I wanted a fifteen-year balloon. What's a good interest rate? How do I pick a neighborhood? What is PMI?

I'm thinking of starting a family of my own someday, and I want to know how to be a good daddy. What should I let my son do? What should I tell him about crossing the street? About sex? How do you remove a splinter without making him cry? How to make him love you more than life itself? I know he'd know the answers, especially to the last one.

So I've been looking. I try to find messages, things he might have left behind to lead me down the right path. I know he thought like that. For months after his death, my mother found flashlights in every room of the house. Big ones, small ones, medium-sized ones, all with fresh batteries. Then she realized: He'd put them there for when he was gone, in case she got scared in the dark, all alone.

Every now and then, I'll discover something prescient. I have the note he left me when I visited him for what turned out to be the last time. There is a quote: "To influence people, appeal to their dreams and aspirations, not just their needs." He wrote in blue ink: "WWT, Jr, We are so glad to have you home for a few days. Love, Daddy."

Or the prayer he read at his last Thanksgiving, when we all still believed. Maybe he knew differently, for he wrote, to himself at the bottom: "What a great prayer for all of us this Thanksgiving day, and for all the tomorrows none of us can take for granted."

But those small whispers and nudges are rare, so I try to find bits of wisdom and the comfort of his presence in the places he loved. I eat at the Mayflower Café in Jackson, Mississippi, I stay at the Hay-Adams Hotel in Washington, D.C., and now, I've come here, to this wonderful, ageless cathedral, walking up and down the perfectly manicured fairways, hoping to find a father. I walk up number ten, crossing fifteen near the grandstand, working back and forth through the pines, making my way toward Amen Corner. He first told me about it. The most amazing place in golf, he'd say reverently. Maybe he'll be here. Maybe he knows his son is lost.

I climb the bleachers, find a spot to sit alone. As I did standing on that rainy night by the small tree, I try to talk to him. There are things I need to ask. How do you be a father? Are you proud of me?

"Daddy," I whisper, "are you out there?"

Something amazing happens. Understand that I don't believe in stuff like this and am certain it is a coincidence . . . but, as the words are leaving my mouth, from across the course, a roar rises from the gallery, breaking the silence, the voices collecting into throaty applause, moving through the pines until it fades away, silence returning to Amen Corner.

◆　◆　◆

Golfers come and go. As the sun warms my face, Jim and Jerry Gray climb the bleachers. They watch a few groups move through and, as they walk away, Jim carefully holds the rope up so his father can slip beneath it. It's a touching moment, something a good son should do for his dad.

Watching this, I realize something. Although I relate to Jim, I also hope that someday, my boy will do the same for me. It's the way with fathers and sons. The hole in your chest after losing your daddy never gets filled. You don't get a new father. You become one yourself, and my transition from son to father is nearing completion.

I walk back. As the clubhouse gets bigger on the horizon, I see a dad and his boy standing near the tenth fairway. Both are wearing golf clothes. I see myself in that father, hoping he can mold his boy as his own daddy molded him.

It occurs to me that all my questions have already been answered. I've been shown how to be a daddy. I just need to throw passes a little long so he'll have to dive. I need to make sure he doesn't lose his stuffed animal, and I need to take him fishing and I need to make him promise not to tell Mama. I need to make sure he knows that you catch more flies with honey than with vinegar and that if it feels wrong, it is. I need to watch *The Guns of Navarone* with him. And I need him to lie next to me, on our tumbuckets, as I explain about a golf tournament in April in Georgia, about Amen Corner and Jack Nicklaus and I need to tell little Walter Wright Thompson III that his grandfather was a great, great man.

◆ ◆ ◆

The clubhouse is in front of me now, and I have one final task. Once I bought my Daddy shirts and windbreakers. On this afternoon, I have something different in mind. I hurry into the cavernous golf shop, past the framed posters and women's clothes to the back of the store. This is unfamiliar territory. I search the wall for the things I want, and I ask the clerk to take them down.

I buy a tiny green Masters onesie, then I pick out a small knit golf shirt, for a toddler. I have one just like it, so, someday in the next few years, when I finally become a father myself and contine this timeless cycle, my son (daughter) can have a connection to this place that's meant so much to me.

At the counter, the woman takes off the tags. When she sees the cute little clothes, she coos. Her words make me hopeful.

"Oh," she gushes, "good daddy!"

Wright Thompson is a senior writer for ESPN.com and ESPN The Magazine. He lives with his wife, Sonia, in Oxford, Mississippi, just up the road from where he grew up. His father, Walter Thompson, was an attorney in Clarksdale, Mississippi. He was always so proud of his boys and would have sent the book in your hands to every single human being he ever met.

Sporting Chance

◆

LEW SCHNEIDER

I can't speak for all fathers of boys—Oh, sure I can. The birth of a son is an opportunity to create an improved version of ourselves. We know what mistakes were made and what opportunities were squandered by our fathers. The arrival of my first son, Marty, gave me a chance to show the world just how great a man I was supposed to have been. One of my first challenges was to turn him into the athlete I had never had the remotest chance of becoming.

Participation in sports is, for better or worse, the chief currency of boyhood. Arrive at a new school and make a diving catch for touchdown at your first recess and you're guaranteed a great table in the cafeteria until graduation. It's like having a black Amex. It's not that I was lousy at sports when I was a kid. I'd had my share of athletic success. There were a number of games where I scored winning baskets, runs, or goals. The problem was, this mostly happened at a Jewish summer camp. Only there could a five-foot-tall guard follow his own missed jump shot and put the rebound up and in. As I entered high school, puberty just barely brushed me as it went by on its way to the non-Jews, who filled out completely by the end of ninth grade. I was badly overmatched when it came to competing for real playing time in the high-profile sports, the ones the girls would go to watch. I wanted better for my son.

Marty has physical advantages that I never had. I did my best to make sure he'd be tall. I wouldn't say that my choice of a spouse was completely based on my desire to produce imposing physical specimens, but the fact that my wife, Liz, is a giantess who had been recruited as a rower when she was applying to college did allow me to overlook the fact that her grandparents felt it foolish to dismiss Hitler as a complete crackpot. It was evident early on that successful breeding had enabled me to break the genetic chain of abuse that had produced generations of tiny liquor salesmen.

With the major physical component in place, it was now up

to me to instill a love of sports and to stoke the boy's competitive fires. I had been so preoccupied with the physical attributes that I ignored what should have been some very red flags in terms of temperament that, in retrospect, show up clearly on both sides of our family. Liz, despite her impressive height, comes from a long line of bookworms. Below her father's high school yearbook photo is the caption "The Guy With the Briefcase." I always figured that, since Liz was graceful and could row and dance, maybe her dad was the genetic anomaly. I should have researched the whole thing more diligently. Liz's grandparents were botanists. In an age when well-heeled collegians rode and swam and boxed, these geeks were out there taking cuttings of ferns and sketching them. On my side, I knew Marty's forebears didn't have much to offer in terms of storied athletic history. Sports, for them, had been limited to long walks across the Russian steppe to avoid conscription in the Czar's Army and, for more intense cardio, fleeing pogroms. By the time they got to this country they were exhausted and busied themselves with retail and gin rummy. Yet, somehow, I had always assumed that there had been latent elite athletes in that group who never got a real opportunity to emerge.

The problem I encountered while fostering Marty's competitive instinct is that the instinct runs counter to the values we try to instill in our children in every other aspect of social development. Put simply, we spend all day telling our toddlers, "Let that boy have a turn" and "Remember to share." Then when it comes time for sports, we expect the kid to put all that aside and GET THAT BALL! Marty was too nice. We could see it when he started playing soccer. If another kid wanted the ball, who was he to make him unhappy? His attitude was, "Oh, you're interested in this? Go, have fun. I'll be watching my shadow and thinking it looks like I'm in a movie."

Even in sports where battling for a loose ball wasn't a main concern, Marty was uninspired. The weakest youth baseball players, the outfielders, can be divided into two categories. They are either "spinners"—kids who like the natural high of dizziness that comes from feeling the wind whizzing past their faces as they twirl around in circles—or they are "diggers"—artistic types who use their cleats and occasionally hands or sticks to carve designs into the outfield turf. Marty was versatile. He was both a brilliant spinner and a digger who, with enough time and space, could create perfectly carved circles that if preserved long enough would, thousands of years from now, surely be regarded as evidence of visits from extraterrestrials. Fearing for Marty's safety—God forbid a line drive should find its way out there and bean him while he was involved in an art project—I'd often holler, "Heads up out there." As we watched, my brother, who actually coached some high school baseball, remarked, "This must be very hard for you." It was excruciating.

When the registration packets arrived for baseball, basketball, soccer, or even roller hockey, Marty always said he wanted to sign up again. "Why?" I asked myself. Unlike most young kids, he was relentlessly agreeable. I'm sure he thought I wanted him to sign up. I didn't want to suggest that he quit, lest I be viewed as the father who had no confidence in his son. And Liz—I'm going to spread the blame a little here—said it was good for him to go out there and exercise and be with other kids. She insisted that it wasn't about whether I thought he was good enough. It was about him having fun, and he said he was. I tried to point out that if he thought he was having fun at sports, imagine what a blast he'd have at something he was able to do. At that point, Liz refused to continue listening, or have sex with me.

Part of the problem was that his crappy performance was being rewarded. People in charge of youth sports today are so preoccupied with making sure everyone participates and is happy that they have forgotten about the poor parents of the lousy player. When you sign up for sports, your kid is guaranteed a trophy. When I was young, you got a trophy when your team won the championship. Now, as long as your parents pay the entry fee, it comes automatically at the end of each season. As if those trophies aren't enough, the coaches, at the obligatory end-of-the-season pizza party, hand out special smaller awards to each kid on the team. Great players are recognized for scoring the most goals or being the best defender. The worst kid, provided he attended practice and didn't bite the other kids, or at least didn't break the skin, wins the sportsmanship award. We have lots of sportsmanship trophies. Marty always had fun at the parties. I'd look over at the team, and Marty would be mixing in quite nicely. The other boys never held his lack of on-field skill against him. He was right in there, talking about goofy characters he'd made up and getting big laughs (with good material, too, not just from cheap fart jokes and messing around with the food). In fact, if they gave a trophy for Best Performance at the Party, he would have won in a cakewalk. So it went, season after season. Marty carted home his prizes at the end without ever cracking the code and realizing he was terrible. Why couldn't a coach just tell him to hang it up? I certainly couldn't. I had to live with him and preserve our healthy relationship.

As boys reach junior high, the more aware among the less skilled players begin to weed themselves out. This occurs at the same time boys develop a sense that other people are watching them. At this age they may also begin changing clothes, or showering, or even combing their hair. Rather than be viewed as lousy athletes, these newly aware types migrate to other activities: drama, music, video-gaming and pre-pot-smoking aimlessness. In this regard, Marty was a late bloomer. In addition to lacking large motor coordination, Marty also lacked the awareness that other people could see him and possibly pass judgment. I have to believe that this deficit comes from his maternal grandfather, "The Guy With the Briefcase." If Grandpa had been aware that others were watching, surely he would have ditched the attaché.

We were up against a ticking clock. The games were getting more serious. I could see that other players looking for someone to pass to would notice that Marty was open, and then look for someone else. Since Marty wasn't paying as close attention as I was, he didn't seem to notice. His attitude seemed to be "I'm here if you need me, but you might want to pass that to someone who really cares." With every on-field miscue I felt the other parents' sideways glances toward Liz and me, the kind that seem to say, "I wonder what those people did to create such a lousy player." To cope, I began making jokes to let the other parents know that I wasn't some clueless fool who didn't understand how vitally important the under-12 soccer games are. Using my keen wit, I let them know I was sympathetic to the plight of the team saddled with the kid who skipped along just behind the action. I quipped, "Wow, look how far away from the ball Marty is. He's missing a real good game out there." Or: "Steven's going to be tired, he's got to cover his guy and Marty's." My sideline bits got mixed reviews. Some of the dads would sort of smile, while many of the moms would both chastise and comfort me by saying, "He's a terrific kid!" (I knew that. He had 20 sportsmanship trophies!) I worried. At some point in the very near future some cruel kid was bound to say, "Hey, you suck." I was then going to have to kill that boy and go to prison for a long time. I couldn't bear the thought. I resolved to tell Marty it was all over.

One day, when Marty was 12, I was driving him to soccer and as we neared the field he asked, "Dad, why should I be hungry?" I said, "What?" He said, "Coach says we should be hungry out there. Why would that help?" I couldn't take it anymore. If Marty couldn't grasp even the most basic sports cliché by now, then, damn it, he was done! I blurted, "Sweetie, there are two more games left, and then we're done with soccer." I quickly caught myself and said, "I mean, if you want to quit after this year, you could. But if you're enjoying it, of course you can keep going."

He looked at me. For a moment I feared there'd be some torrent of emotion, that he'd break down and cry, "Finally! I've only been doing this for you! Oh, Dad, thank you, thank you! Let's go buy me a Stratocaster and some weed!" There was none of that. He just said that sounded good to him and wondered if I'd ever seen *Monty Python's The Meaning of Life.* He then went on to describe all the parts he found particularly amusing.

He didn't quit sports completely. Marty likes to be physically active; he does love to ski and climb. I wondered if maybe it was just the team experience that wasn't engaging him. When his buddy signed up for tennis, Liz asked Marty if maybe he would want to give that a try. Marty, loving the idea of hanging with his pal, enthusiastically agreed.

I drove Marty and Daniel to the first lesson. The two were so completely engrossed in discussions of funny movies and Bill Cosby routines that I had to direct each movement: "Guys, get your rackets. Hey, close the car door. Watch it, that car is pulling out." They finally realized where they were when I introduced them to Eric, the instructor. As they made their way to the court, Marty and Daniel continued chattering away and singing Tom Lehrer songs they'd memorized. From his side of the net, Eric showed them the basic forehand and then proceeded to hit very soft shots for them to return. I watched as Marty swung at and completely missed the first three. Eric was very encouraging. Daniel did a Fat Albert voice and Marty laughed. Marty missed the fourth and then hit the fifth off the racket frame, sending it sideways onto the adjacent court. I called Liz on my cell. She said, "Hello?" I said simply, "It isn't tennis" and hung up.

So it's not tennis. It's not soccer or baseball or basketball or any ball. And as little interest as he has in playing the games, he has even less when it comes to watching. He actually left a Super Bowl party at halftime because he was tired of watching the game and felt that he'd already seen all the funny commercials.

❖　❖　❖

Marty never got it. He would never be even the mediocre athlete I was. If he'd stayed with sports, he'd still be the last player chosen at a Hasidic softball game. What I've got is a comedy geek. That's what he's really into: comedy. Any comedy. Even bad improv. Nowadays he's consumed with making funny videos and posting them on the web. Great. So he's funny. What do you do with that? I just don't see where that's going to get him. I guess you just have to give up at some point and let children find their own way. As long as he's not hurting anyone. As long as he's not the one doing the bad improv.

With my two younger boys I've mellowed a bit. I just don't get as emotionally invested in their athletic endeavors. Naturally, my middle son has turned out to be a really competitive athlete who is a bear to live with. He dissects every baseball game he plays, pitch by pitch. It makes me miss riding home and hearing about what Homer had said to Grandpa Simpson. Nonetheless, it is hard to look at Marty, who is now almost 6'2", and think that he'll never excel in competitive sports. He's got a perfect rower's body. His mom rowed. I'm sure he could row. If I could just convince him that rowing is funny.

Lew Schneider has been a stand-up comedian, kids' game-show host, sitcom regular, television writer/producer, and essayist. He won two Emmy awards for his work on the CBS comedy Everybody Loves Raymond *and was a victorious color war general at Camp Naomi in 1981.*

Dirty Moves

◆

JAMES BROWN

At 4:30 on Sunday morning I roust my boys out of bed and tell them to use the bathroom. When they're done, each takes his turn stepping onto the scale beside the tub. They're groggy, of course. They're slow to react, but they don't protest. My older son understands the importance of a single ounce in wrestling, and the younger is quickly learning. The slightest difference in weight can mean having to compete in the next division, potentially giving away nearly five precious pounds to your opponent. That might not sound like much, but it is when you're already little more than muscle and bone. Stripped to his boxers, Logan tops the scale at 111. He's a pound and one ounce over the weight for the division in which he prefers to wrestle, where he's strongest, between 105 and 109. Logan curses, the most popular four-letter expletive in the book.

"Don't cuss," I say, though his father is hardly a model of civil speech.

Logan steps off the scale.

"I knew I shouldn't have eaten that banana last night," he says.

"You might still make it."

"How?"

"By the time we get there," I say, "you'll probably have to use the bathroom again. That's another three, maybe four ounces. And you can always run around the gym a couple times."

At twelve, Logan has been wrestling competitively for five years, and he does not like even the slightest disadvantage. Little Nate, on the other hand, is only six and weighs in at thirty-four and a half pounds, close to the limit for his class. I pat him on the head as he steps off the scale.

"Good going," I say.

"What?"

"You're on weight."

"Oh," he says. "Is that good?"

"It's very good."

This is his first year in competition, and he's excited, wanting to follow in his brother's footsteps and win his own shelf full of medals and trophies. I'm confident that he will. The youngest in the brood is often the toughest, having on a daily basis to fight off the tortures and teasing of his older brothers.

By five we're in the car, headed for El Monte High School in the San Gabriel Valley. It's a good seventy miles or better, and we need to be there between six and seven for weigh-ins. Miss those and you don't wrestle. Nate is snuggled in the back with a blanket and a pillow. Logan sits shotgun but with the seat reclined, huddled under his Levi's jacket, so that he too can sleep while I drive. I sip coffee and try to keep my eyes open. It's still dark, and fortunately there aren't many people on the road. We make good time. Shortly after sunrise, we pull off the freeway, drive a few more miles, and then turn into the parking lot of the high school. Already it's beginning to fill up.

The registration tables are situated outside the main entrance to the gym. I get in line with the other parents and wait my turn with Nate. Logan, meanwhile, takes this opportunity to run around the gym, hoping to shed those last ounces. A few minutes later I step up to the table and show the woman in charge my kids' USA Wrestling cards.

"What team are they on?"

"We're independent."

"Excuse me?"

"We don't have a team," I say. "It's just me and my two sons."

"I'm sorry, sir," she says. "They have to be on a registered USA team or they can't wrestle."

We used to have a team but it disbanded a couple of years back when the coach's three boys graduated from USA Wrestling's youth programs to high school wrestling. Now, from time to time, especially when the people working the registration tables are new to their job, I have problems. But I'm prepared. I know the bylaws by heart, down to the page stating that independents are allowed to compete as long as they're accompanied by a registered Copper Coach with a current Copper Coach card. And that person would be me. I'm about to rattle all this off to the woman when the man working the table beside her, a man who's registered us several times in the past, speaks up.

"No, we take independents. We don't get many, but we take them. I know this guy," he says. "You're from the mountains, right?"

"Lake Arrowhead."

He whistles.

"Long drive," he says.

Once I've signed them in and paid the entry fees, I search out Logan, catching him as he rounds the corner of the gym at an even jog. He's worked up a sweat, though he's not breathing heavily, the sign of an athlete in shape.

"Did you use the bathroom?" I ask.

"Yeah, but I barely had to go."

I look at my watch.

"Better quit running," I say. "There's only twenty minutes left for weigh-ins."

"I don't think I'll make it."

"So you wrestle up a division. It's no big deal," I say. "You're tough."

"Yeah," he says. "Except that kid from Norwalk goes one-tens."

He's referring to the boy who beat him for first place at an earlier tournament. It was a close match, Logan leading by two points going into the last round when he took a chance, made an error, and the other kid capitalized on it.

I try to be upbeat. I try to turn his self-doubt around on him.

"That's good," I tell him.

"Why?"

"Because you need the competition. You learn more from your losses, not your wins. Besides, you'll get him this time."

Gang graffiti mars the walls of the boys' locker room, and the lockers themselves are mostly busted and broken. This is where weigh-ins take place, and it's packed with kids from the competing teams. The Outkasts. The Terminators. Fontana Boyz and the Scorpions. All have team warm-up suits while my sons are simply dressed in jeans and T-shirts. Clearly we stand out, and not solely for lack of uniforms. We are one of the few white families in an overwhelmingly Mexican-American community. I don't know if it's my imagination or not, if I invite it somehow, or if it's just part and parcel to the nature of this sport, but we occasionally get that dirty, lingering look that suggests we're not welcome here.

In the last ten years or so, wrestling also has become more popular with girls, which is terrific, but because of their presence in the locker room—and there are only a few here this morning—it's mandatory that the boys weigh in wearing their wrestling singlets. For Logan, that means forsaking another couple of ounces, and sure enough, when he strips down to his singlet and steps on the scale, he's over the mark.

The man working the scale jots down Logan's weight on a clipboard. Then he writes "110 ½" on my son's arm with a black felt-tip pen. Next in line is Nate, and he's been watching his brother. He knows to wait until the man signals him to step forward, and I admire this about him, that at six he's already well-mannered and mindful of his surroundings. He weighs in at thirty-four pounds, meaning he'll wrestle thirties. The divisions are separated by five-pound increments.

As my boys are putting their clothes back on, I notice Logan staring at something, his eyes narrowed. I look in the same direction. The kid from Norwalk is staring back at him, just as meanly, from the other end of the locker room. I put my hand on Logan's shoulder, which seems to break the spell.

"What're you doing?"

"He's trying to psyche me out."

"Don't go there with him," I say. "Don't let him rattle you."

"I'll kick his ass."

"You're here to wrestle," I tell him, "not fight. That's exactly what he wants you to do—lose your temper and screw up."

But I can see he's not listening. I know my son well. We're very much alike in temperament, quick to anger, and when he gets like this it's impossible to reach him. For better or worse, and I suspect it's for the worse, this ugly thing will just have to run its course.

The younger children, between the ages of five and eleven, wrestle in the morning. The older ones, twelve to fifteen, compete in the afternoon. In Nate's first match he goes up against a tough little kid from nearby Fontana, birthplace of that fun-loving fraternity known as the Hells Angels. Because I am a card-carrying Copper Coach who has paid all the necessary fees and dues and attended all the mandatory seminars, I'm allowed in my son's corner on the mat. The other fathers and mothers have to stand on the sidelines, which are cordoned off with yellow caution tape, and watch the team coach instruct their sons and daughters. I hand the bout sheet to the scorekeepers and then take Nate aside. He's nervous, shifting his weight from one foot to the other. I kneel down so we're looking eye-to-eye.

"What's the game plan?"

"Go for points," he says. "Don't worry about the pin."

Those are my exact words.

"What else?"

"Just relax," he says, "and do my best."

"Good."

The teenage referee, likely a volunteer from the high school's wrestling team, calls Nate out to the mat. I give him a pat on the back, a gentle nudge to get him moving. The other kid is waiting for him. He's crouched over, his knees slightly bent, hands out to his sides. It's the proper stance. Nate assumes the same position. They shake hands and then the ref blows the whistle.

It's hard to imagine brutality among six-year-olds. It's hard to imagine how a coach, or a father, could in good conscience teach a child to inflict pain on another child in a fair and clean sport. But in the first round the Fontana boy tries to bend Nate's arm, and when he can't do it, because Nate is holding strong, he strikes him in the crook of the elbow. Once. Twice. Three times. The ref is slow to respond, and when he finally does, when he stops it, it's not even with a penalty. Then, in the second round, the kid grabs Nate from behind, locking his arms around Nate's waist. Leaning back, lifting him into the air, he slams my boy face down into the mat.

I see him squint in pain.

I see him fight back the tears and I want it stopped. Right now. This is not what wrestling is about. This is not how I've taught my kids. Slamming also merits a penalty for unnecessary roughness, but the ref again fails to note it. I'm a second away from calling the match when I see it, this glint in Nate's eye, his face suddenly hardened with resolve. The boy is on top of him, and Nate locks the kid's arm under his own and rolls him, perfectly, onto his back for a one-point reversal and three point near-fall. The round ends a moment later, and Nate returns to his corner.

I drop to one knee, so he can hear me better.

"You're doing great. That kid's a dirty wrestler but you're smarter, you're faster. This is the last round," I say, "and you're behind by two points. I want you to go for the takedowns. Don't worry about anything else. He's leading too far with the left leg and that's what you want. That left leg. After you take him down, let him back up, OK?"

"Let him back up?"

"Right."

"What for?"

"Because you're going to take him down again. Only the second time, I want you to hang on, just ride him out till it's over. Escapes are only worth one point and takedowns are worth two, and you're going to win this match by one point."

And that's what he does.

When the match is over, Nate walks off the mat victorious, smiling proudly. Unfortunately his next couple of bouts are even tougher, though by no means as violent as the first. He loses two by narrow margins but wins his last by a pin and earns himself a fifth-place ribbon out of the twelve in his division. Not bad for his first tournament. Logan wrestles later that afternoon, winning three in a row and qualifying for the final bout for first or second place in the 110 weight class. His opponent, of course, is the boy from Norwalk, who also has won three in a row, all pins.

In Logan's corner, as I'm rubbing his arms, loosening him up, I tell him pretty much what I told his brother.

"Go for the takedowns. Go for rolls and reversals. If the pin presents itself, great. But this kid is strong. Don't butt heads with him."

"I'm stronger."

"You probably are," I say, though I'm not so sure. "I want to see some good smart wrestling out there, not some brawl."

Unlike street fighting, there are rules here. The intent is not to injure, and moves like arm-bars and chokeholds are taboo. Wrestling is about controlling your opponent, not destroying him, and I try to instill in my sons a sense of principle and respect for the sport. For Logan, fixated on avenging his narrow loss, it's a tough sale today, and I'm worried when the ref calls him out to the mat. I'm worried that this could turn into a free-for-all.

The ref hands him a strip of red Velcro, which Logan wraps around his ankle, identifying him for the scorekeepers. The kid from Norwalk hustles out, waving his arms, doing a kind of goose step. He's cocky. He's arrogant, and I want it even more now, for Logan to beat him, to knock that ego down a few notches. If nothing else, it would serve the kid well later in life.

They shake hands.

The ref blows the whistle and Logan shoots in, not wasting a second, catching the boy off guard and taking him down for two quick points. I'm on the sidelines, excited now.

"All right," I shout. "Now turn him. Get him on his back."

In the heat of battle, and given the headgear that wrestlers wear to protect their ears, I doubt if he hears anything I say. Of course that doesn't stop me from trying, and I continue to shout instructions from the sidelines, as does the opposing coach, a stout, potbellied man with a goatee. The kid escapes and gets to his feet, but not before Logan rocks him onto his back, scoring a near-fall for another three points. The first round ends with my boy leading five to one. Logan returns to his corner breathing hard.

I hug him.

"Good work," I say. "Another takedown and that'll put you ahead seven to one. Lock him up. Ride him through the second round. Got that?"

Logan nods.

"Keep that lead going into the third," I say, "and it's over."

The rest period ends. Logan returns to the mat, and about halfway through the second round he scores yet another take-down. I suck in a deep breath. I let it out slowly. Assuming he doesn't get pinned, there's no way that the other kid can catch up. He's done it. He's won, and I'm proud of him. That he didn't lose his cool. That he wrestled smart.

Then something happens. Something bad.

The kid works himself free. The kid scrambles to his feet, and I don't believe that what happens next is an accident. I don't believe that his hand catching in my son's headgear is an inno-cent mistake, any more than I do his pulling the straps down

175

across Logan's eyes, blinding him. Why the ref doesn't call it for what it is—a blatant foul—is beyond me. Logan takes it for granted, as any good wrestler might, that the ref will shout for a time-out, and it costs him, this assumption, this belief that sport is fair. It's a disappointing but necessary lesson, and I blame myself that Logan has to learn it this way, for not having taught him earlier that in sport, as in life, you must often assume the worst in another.

Dazed, confused, he stands up straight, and the other kid rushes him, like a lineman taking out a quarterback. He rams him in the stomach. As his back strikes the mat I actually hear the swell of air forced from his lungs, and inside of five seconds the referee blows the whistle. Logan has been pinned. He gets to his feet and rips off the red Velcro strip from around his ankle and throws it in the ref's face. That's when I snap, when the other coach, the guy with the goatee, starts screaming at my son.

"You apologize," he says.

"Go to hell," Logan says.

He steps toward my son, but I'm there now, between them.

"You discipline your kid," I say, "I'll discipline mine."

"Your boy's a sore loser."

"Your boy's a cheater."

For a few seconds we just stare each other down. I know I've crossed a line I should never cross, especially in front of my children, but how much can you reasonably take before you lose it? He turns away, and it's good that one of us does it.

On the ride home that afternoon I ask my sons what they would like for dinner. "Anything," I say. "You name it." This is tradition. This is my offer after every tournament, win or lose, as a reward for a day well spent together. Typically, from Logan anyway, it invites a single word—steak, say, or shrimp. He loves both. And I love to cook either for them. Today, however, when I pop the question, I receive no answer. I look at Nate in the rearview mirror. Already a welt is forming above his left eye—the result, I imagine, of a well-placed elbow or knee to the face, a blow I hadn't noticed. His arm, where the first kid struck him, is also bruised and sore. I watch him rub it. I watch him bend it up and down, slowly, like it must hurt.

"How about you, Nate?" I say. "Want anything special for dinner?"

All I get is a shrug.

For a while I let it go. For a while we drive in silence. Logan is pretty beat up, too, with bruised ribs where that kid speared him, and, from another bout, scratches on his neck and down one side of his face. I wonder if it's worth it, if maybe it's time to hang it up. I don't want to ask the question, because it's always been my favorite sport, because I live through my kids, as parents often do, but it seems the right thing now.

"Maybe we should try something else," I say. "Like soccer. Or baseball."

"What are you talking about?" Logan says.

"We don't have to wrestle, you know. There are other sports."

"No way," he says. "I'm nailing that stupid Mexican next time."

Half my childhood was spent in Los Angeles, the other half in East San Jose. My stepmother is Mexican. My stepbrother and stepsister are Mexican, and two of my lifelong best friends are Mexican, one so close to the family the boys call him uncle. Uncle Orlando. I've experienced hate, and I've experienced the sort of acceptance and love that transcends it. My son, I think, ought to know better. I raise my voice.

"What'd you just say?"

He bows his head.

"Nothing," he says.

"I don't want to hear you talk like that again. You understand me? No more cussing, either. I've had it." He's quiet. I shake my head. I look at him again, hard. "You're mad because he cheated. That's it. That's all. Don't get it mixed up. Mexican has nothing to do with it."

I would like to believe my own words, and I do. I would like to believe that I can offer my sons a better world where there is no racism, no cheaters, no parents who teach their children to hate and hurt others. But I can offer them no such thing. At best I can only instruct so that they might suffer less, and so that in surviving they know when to suspend the rules, for their own protection. As we drive home that evening, both boys staring silently out the window, bruised and shaken, I make them a promise.

We will have steak tonight.

We will have shrimp, too. The works. And afterward, when calm has prevailed, I will lead them to the middle of the living room floor and lovingly show them the moves I eventually had to learn, those dirty ones, the kind designed to hurt.

James Brown is the author of The Los Angeles Diaries: A Memoir, *several novels, and a collection of short stories. His essays have appeared in the* Los Angeles Times Magazine, The New York Times Magazine, *and* GQ. *He's received a National Endowment for the Arts grant in Fiction Writing and the Nelson Algren Award for Short Fiction.* The Los Angeles Diaries: A Memoir *was selected as one of the "Best Books of the Year" by* Publishers Weekly, *the* San Francisco Chronicle, *and* The Independent *in the U.K. Brown teaches at California State University, San Bernardino and lives with his family in Lake Arrowhead, California.*

Mailer vs. Mailer

◆

JOHN BUFFALO MAILER

By the time I was born, boxing had become the family sport. My father and his friends, my brothers and their friends, and my cousin and his friends went to the Gramercy Gym every Saturday morning, back in the early eighties, to spar. There existed an understanding that usually worked: they were not there to beat the piss out of each other, but to learn a little about themselves. Some may disagree, but in my father's world, boxing is truly one of the arts. This belief was fortified by the presence on most Saturdays of José Torres, who had been the light-heavyweight champion in the sixties.

I was four years old at the time, but my dad let me come along on Saturdays and once even put me in the ring. Although I was considerably outsized by the forty-year-old man in the opposite corner, I had already come to the understanding that, when your time came, you just had to fight.

Of course, I was in no danger. However, someone happened to take a picture over the shoulder of the man in the opposite corner, capturing the look of terror in my four-year-old eyes. The expression on my face—I thought I was really going to have to fight this man—makes me smile even to this day, and I imagine gave the guys at the club no end of amusement. It was not unlike the time my dad got down on his knees to box with me in our living room. I had just turned three at the time. He let me catch him one on the corner of his chin and immediately dropped to the floor, pretending I had knocked him out. I had, for a few hours, the gift of believing I possessed the best right hook in the world.

John Buffalo Mailer is the Director of Development for Tar Films, the film and documentary division of Tar Art Media. While still in college, Mailer published his first novella, Hello Herman. Mailer was Executive Editor of High Times magazine from 2004–2005. He is the co-author of The Big Empty—a book of discussions between him and his father, Norman Mailer.

A River Runs Through It

◆

NORMAN MACLEAN

As a Scot and a Presbyterian, my father believed that man by nature was a mess and had fallen from an original state of grace. Somehow, I early developed the notion that he had done this by falling from a tree. As for my father, I never knew whether he believed God was a mathematician, but he certainly believed God could count and that only by picking up God's rhythms were we able to regain power and beauty. Unlike many Presbyterians, he often used the word "beautiful."

After he buttoned his glove, he would hold his rod straight out in front of him, where it trembled with the beating of his heart. Although it was eight and a half feet long, it weighed only four and a half ounces. It was made of split bamboo cane from the far-off Bay of Tonkin. It was wrapped with red and blue silk thread, and the wrappings were carefully spaced to make the delicate rod powerful but not so stiff it could not tremble.

Always it was to be called a rod. If someone called it a pole, my father looked at him as a sergeant in the United States Marines would look at a recruit who had just called a rifle a gun.

My brother and I would have preferred to start learning how to fish by going out and catching a few, omitting entirely anything difficult or technical in the way of preparation that would take away from the fun. But it wasn't by way of fun that we were introduced to our father's art. If our father had had his say, nobody who did not know how to fish would be allowed to disgrace a fish by catching him. So you too will have to approach the art Marine- and Presbyterian-style, and, if you have never picked up a fly rod before, you will soon find it factually and theologically true that man by nature is a damn mess. The four-and-a-half-ounce thing in silk wrappings that trembles with the underskin motions of the flesh becomes a stick without brains, refusing anything simple that is wanted of it. All that a rod has to do is lift the line, the leader, and the fly off the water, give them a good toss over the head, and then shoot them forward so they will land in the water without a splash in the following order: fly, transparent leader, and then the line—otherwise the fish will see the fly is a fake and be gone. Of course, there are special casts that anyone could predict would be difficult, and they require artistry—casts where the line can't go over the fisherman's head because cliffs or trees are immediately behind, sideways casts to get the fly under overhanging willows, and so on. But what's remarkable about just a straight cast—just picking up a rod with line on it and tossing the line across the river?

Well, until man is redeemed he will always take a fly rod too far back, just as natural man always overswings with an ax or golf club and loses all his power somewhere in the air; only with a rod it's worse, because the fly often comes so far back it gets caught behind in a bush or rock. When my father said it was an art that ended at two o'clock, he often added, "closer to twelve than to two," meaning that the rod should be taken back only slightly farther than overhead (straight overhead being twelve o'clock).

Then, since it is natural for man to try to attain power without recovering grace, he whips the line back and forth making it whistle each way, and sometimes even snapping off the fly from the leader, but the power that was going to transport the little fly across the river somehow gets diverted into building a bird's nest of line, leader, and fly that falls out of the air into the water about ten feet in front of the fisherman. If, though, he pictures the round trip of the line, transparent leader, and fly from the time they leave the water until their return, they are easier in cast. They naturally come off the water heavy line first and in front, and light transparent leader and fly trailing behind. But, as they pass over-head, they have to have a little beat of time so the light, transpar-ent leader and fly from the time the leave the water until their return, they are easier to cast. They naturally come off the water heavy line first and in front, and light transparent leader and fly trailing behind. But, as they pass overhead, they have to have a lit-tle beat of time so the light, transparent leader and fly can catch up to the heavy line now starting forward and again fall behind it; otherwise, the line starting on its return trip will collide with the leader and fly still on their way up, and the mess will be the bird's nest that splashes into the water ten feel in front of the fisherman.

Almost the moment, however, that the forward order of line, leader, and fly is reestablished, it has to be reversed, because the fly and transparent leader must be ahead of the heavy line when they settle on the water. If what the fish sees is highly visible line, what the fisherman will see are departing black darts, and he might as well start for the next hole. High overhead, then, on the forward cast (at about ten o'clock) the fisherman checks again.

The four-count rhythm, of course, is functional. The one count takes the line, leader, and fly off the water; the two count tosses them seemingly straight into the sky: the three count was my father's way of saying that at the top the leader and fly have to be given a little beat of time to get behind the line as it is starting forward; the four count means put on the power and throw the line into the rod until you reach ten o'clock—then check-cast, let the fly and leader get ahead of the line, and coast to a soft and perfect landing. Power comes not from power everywhere, but from knowing where to put it on. "Remember," as my father kept saying, "it is an art that is performed on a four-count rhythm between ten and two o'clock."

My father was very sure about certain matters pertaining to the universe. To him, all good things—trout as well as eternal salvation—come by grace and grace comes by art and art does not come easy.

So my brother and I learned to cast Presbyterian-style, on a metronome. It was mother's metronome, which father had taken from the top of the piano in town. She would occasionally peer down to the dock from the front porch of the cabin, wondering nervously whether her metronome could float if it had to. When she became so overwrought that she thumped down the dock to reclaim it, my father would clap out the four-count rhythm with his cupped hands.

Eventually, he introduced us to literature on the subject. He tried always to say something stylish as he buttoned the glove on his casting hand. "Izaak Walton," he told us when my brother was thirteen or fourteen, "is not a respectable writer. He was an Episcopalian and a bait fisherman." Although Paul was three years younger than I was, he was already far ahead of me in anything relating to fishing, and it was he who first found a copy of *The Compleat Angler* and reported back to me. "The bastard doesn't even know how to spell 'complete.' Besides, he has songs to sing to dairymaids." I borrowed his copy, and reported back to him, "Some of those songs are pretty good." He said, "Whoever saw a dairymaid on the Big Blackfoot River?"

My father and mother were in retirement now, and neither one liked "being out of things," especially my mother, who was younger than my father and was used to "running the church." To them, Paul was the reporter, their chief contact with reality, the recorder of the world that was leaving them and that they had never known very well anyway. He had to tell them story after story, even though they did not approve of some of them. We sat around the table a long time. As we started to get up, I said to Father, "We'd appreciate it if you would go fishing with us tomorrow."

"Oh," my father said and sat down again, automatically unfolded his napkin, and asked, "Are you sure, Paul, that you want me? I can't fish some of those big holes anymore. I can't wade anymore."

Paul said, "Sure I want you. Whenever you can get near fish, you can catch them."

To my father, the highest commandment was to do whatever his sons wanted him to do, especially if it meant to go fishing. The minister looked as if his congregation had just asked him to come back and preach his farewell sermon over again.

It was getting to be after their bedtime, and it had been a long day for Paul and me. So I thought I'd help Mother with the dishes and then we'd turn in for the night. But I really knew that things weren't going to be that simple, and they knew it, too. Paul gave himself a stretch as soon as it was not immediately after dinner, and said, "I think I'll run over town and see some old pals. I'll be back before long, but don't wait up for me."

I helped my mother with the dishes. Although only one had left, all the voices had gone. He had stayed long enough after dinner for us to think he would be happy spending an evening at home. Each of us knew some of his friends, and all of us knew his favorite pal, who was big and easy and nice to us, especially to Mother. He had just got out of prison. His second stretch.

From the time my mother stood looking at the closed doors until she went to bed, she said only. "Goodnight." She said it over her shoulder near the head of the stairs to both my father and me.

I never could tell how much my father knew about my brother. I generally assumed that he knew a good deal because there is a substantial minority in every church congregation who regard it as their Christian duty to keep the preacher informed about the preacher's kids. Also, at times, my father would start to talk to me about Paul as if he were going to open up a new subject and then he would suddenly put a lid on it before the subject spilled out.

"Did you hear what Paul did lately?" he asked.

I told him, "I don't understand you. I hear all kinds of things about Paul. Mostly, I hear he's a fine reporter and a fine fisherman."

"No, no," my father said. "But haven't you heard what he does afterwards?"

I shook my head.

Then I think he had another thought about what he was thinking, and swerved from what he was going to say. "Haven't you heard," he asked me, "that he has changed his spelling of our name from Maclean to MacLean. Now he spells it with a capital L."

"Oh, sure," I said. "I knew all about that. He told me he got tired of nobody spelling his name right. They even wrote his paychecks with a capital L, so he finally decided to give up and spell his name the way others do."

My father shook his head at my explanation, its truth being irrelevant. He murmured both to himself and to me, "It's a terrible thing to spell our name with a capital L. Now somebody will think we are Scottish Lowlanders and not Islanders."

He went to the door and looked out and when he came back he didn't ask me any questions. He tried to tell me. He spoke in the abstract, but he had spent his life fitting abstractions to listeners so that listeners would have no trouble fitting his abstractions to the particulars of their lives.

"You are too young to help anybody and I am too old," he said. "By help I don't mean a courtesy like serving choke-cherry jelly or giving money.

"Help," he said, "is giving part of yourself to somebody who comes to accept it willingly and needs it badly.

"So it is," he said, using an old homiletic transition, "that we can seldom help anybody. Either we don't know what part to give or maybe we don't like to give any part of ourselves. Then, more often than not, the part that is needed is not wanted. And even more often, we do not have the part that is needed. It is like the auto-supply shop over town where they always say, 'Sorry, we are just out of that part.'"

I told him, "You make it too tough. Help doesn't have to be anything that big."

He asked me, "Do you think your mother helps him by buttering his rolls?"

"She might," I told him. "In fact, yes, I think she does."

"Do you think you help him?" he asked me.

"I try to," I said. "My trouble is I don't know him. In fact, one of my troubles is that I don't even know whether he needs help. I don't know, that's my trouble."

"That should have been my text," my father said. "We are willing to help, Lord, but what if anything is needed?

"I still know how to fish," he concluded. "Tomorrow we will go fishing with him."

I lay waiting a long time before finally falling asleep. I felt the rest of the upstairs was also waiting.

Usually, I get up early to observe the commandment observed by only some of us—to arise early to see as much of the Lord's daylight as is given to us. I several times heard my brother open my door, study my covers, and then close my door. I began waking up by remembering that my brother, no matter what, was never late for work or fishing. One step closer to waking and I remembered that this was the trip when my brother was taking care of me. Now it began to seep into me that he was making my breakfast, and, when this became a matter of knowledge, I got up and dressed. All three were sitting at the table, drinking tea and waiting.

Mother said, as if she had wakened to find herself Queen for a Day. "Paul made breakfast for us." This made him feel good enough to smile early in the morning, but when he was serving me I looked closely and could see the blood vessels in his eyes. A fisherman, though, takes a hangover as a matter of course—after a couple of hours of fishing, it goes away, all except the dehydration, but then he is standing all day in water.

We somehow couldn't get started that morning. After Paul and I had left home. Father put away his fishing tackle, probably thinking he was putting it away for good, so now he couldn't remember where. Mother had to find most of the things for him. She knew nothing about fishing or fishing tackle, but she knew how to find things, even when she did not know what they looked like.

Paul, who usually got everyone nervous by being impatient to be on the stream, kept telling Father, "Take it easy. It's turned cooler. We'll make a killing today. Take it easy" But my father, from whom my brother had inherited his impatience to have his flies on water, would look at me visibly loathing himself for being old and not able to collect himself.

My mother had to go from basement to attic and to most closets in between looking for a fishing basket while she made lunches for three men, each of whom wanted a different kind of sandwich. After she got us in the car, she checked each car door to see that none of her men would fall out. Then she dried her hands in her apron, although her hands were not wet, and said, "Thank goodness," as we drove away.

I was at the wheel, and I knew before we started just where we were going. It couldn't be far up the Blackfoot, because we were starting late, and it had to be a stretch of water of two or three deep holes for Paul and me and one good hole with no bank too steep for Father to crawl down. Also, since he couldn't wade, the good fishing water had to be on his side of the river. They argued while I drove, although they knew just as well as I did where we had to go, but each one in our family considered himself the leading authority on how to fish the Blackfoot River. When we came to the side road going to the river above the mouth of Belmont Creek, they spoke in unison for the first time. "Turn here," they said, and, as if I were following their directions, I turned to where I was going anyway.

The side road brought us down to a flat covered with ground boulders and cheat grass. No livestock grazed on it, and grasshoppers took off like birds and flew great distances, because on this flat it is a long way between feeding grounds, even for grasshoppers. The flat itself and its crop of boulders are the roughly ground remains of one of geology's great disasters. The flat may well have been the end of the ice-age lake, half as big as Lake Michigan, that in places was two thousand feet deep until the glacial dam broke and this hydraulic monster of the hills charged out onto the plains of eastern Washington. High on the mountains above where we stopped to fish are horizontal scars slashed by passing icebergs.

I had to be careful driving toward the river so I wouldn't high-center the car on a boulder and break the crankcase. The flat ended suddenly and the river was down a steep bank, blinking silver through the trees and then turning to blue by comparing itself to a red and green cliff. It was another world to see and feel, and another world of rocks. The boulders on the flat were shaped by the last ice age only eighteen or twenty thousand years ago, but the red and green precambrian rocks beside the blue water were almost from the basement of the world and time.

We stopped and peered down the bank. I asked my father, "Do you remember when we picked a lot of red and green rocks down there to build our fireplace? Some were red mudstones with ripples on them."

"Some had raindrops on them," he said. His imagination was always stirred by the thought that he was standing in ancient rain spattering on mud before it became rocks.

"Nearly a billion years ago," I said, knowing what he was thinking.

He paused. He had given up the belief that God had created all there was, Including the Blackfoot River, on a six-day work schedule, but he didn't believe that the job so taxed God's powers that it took Him forever to complete.

"Nearly *half* a billion years ago." he said as his contribution to reconciling science and religion. He hurried on, not wishing to waste any part of old age in debate, except over fishing. "We carried those big rocks up the bank," he said, "but now I can't crawl down it. Two holes below, though, the river comes out in the open and there is almost no bank. I'll walk down there and fish, and you fish the first two holes. I'll wait in the sun. Don't hurry."

Paul said, "You'll get them," and all of a sudden father was confident in himself again. Then he was gone.

We could catch glimpses of him walking along the bank of the river which had been the bottom of the great glacial lake. He held his rod straight in front of him and every now and then he lunged forward with it, perhaps reenacting some glacial race memory in which he speared a hairy ice age mastodon and ate him for breakfast.

Paul said. "Let's fish together today," I knew then that he was still taking care of me because we almost always split up when we fished. "That's fine," I said. "I'll wade across and fish the other side," he said. I said, "Fine," again, and was doubly touched. On the other side you were backed against cliffs and trees, so it was mostly a roll-casting job, never my specialty. Besides, the river was power-ful here with no good place to wade, and next to fishing Paul liked swimming rivers with his rod in his hand. It turned out he didn't have to swim here, but as he waded sometimes the wall of water rose to his upstream shoulder while it would be no higher than his hip behind him. He stumbled to shore from the weight of water in his clothes, and gave me a big wave.

I came down the bank to catch fish. Cool wind had blown in from Canada without causing any electric storms, so the fish should be off the bottom and feeding again. When a deer comes to water, his head shoots in and out of his shoulders to see what's ahead, and I was looking all around to see what fly to put on. But I didn't have to look further than my neck or my nose. Big clumsy flies bumped into my face, swarmed on my neck and wiggled in my underwear. Blundering and soft-bellied, they had been born before they had brains. They had spent a year under water on legs, had crawled out on a rock, had become flies and copulated with the ninth and tenth segments of their abdomens, and then had died as the first light wind blew them into the water where the fish circled excitedly. They were a fish's dream come true—stupid, succulent, and exhausted from copulation. Still, it would be hard to know what gigantic portion of human life is spent in this same ratio of years under water on legs to one premature, exhausted moment on wings.

✦ ✦ ✦

Father probably was already waiting for us. Paul threw his cigarette in the water and was gone without seeing whether I landed the fish.

Not only was I on the wrong side of the river to fish with drowned stone flies, but Paul was a good enough roll caster to have already fished most of my side from his own. But I caught two more. They also started as little circles that looked like little fish feeding on the surface but were broken arches of big rainbows under water. After I caught these two, I quit. They made ten, and the last three were the finest fish I ever caught. They weren't the biggest or most spectacular fish I ever caught, but they were three fish I caught because my brother waded across the river to give me the fly that would catch them and because they were the last fish I ever caught fishing with him.

After cleaning my fish. I set these three apart with a layer of grass and wild mint.

Then I lifted the heavy basket, shook myself into the shoulder strap until it didn't cut any more, and thought, "I'm through for the day. I'll go down and sit on the bank by my father and talk." Then I added, "If he doesn't feel like talking, I'll just sit."

I could see the sun ahead. The coming burst of light made it look from the shadows that I and a river inside the earth were about to appear on earth. Although I could as yet see only the sunlight and not anything in it. I knew my father was sitting somewhere on the bank. I knew partly because he and I shared many of the same impulses, even to quitting at about the same time. I was sure without as yet being able to see into what was in front of me that he was sitting somewhere in the sunshine reading the New Testament in Greek. I knew this both from instinct and experience.

Old age had brought him moments of complete peace. Even when we went duck hunting and the roar of the early morning shooting was over, he would sit in the blind wrapped in an old army blanket with his Greek New Testament in one hand and his shotgun in the other. When a stray duck happened by, he would drop the book and raise the gun, and, after the shooting was over, he would raise the book again, occasionally interrupting his reading to thank his dog for retrieving the duck.

The voices of the subterranean river in the shadows were different from the voices of the sunlit river ahead. In the shadows against the cliff the river was deep and engaged in profundities, circling back on itself now and then to say things over to be sure it had understood itself. But the river ahead came out into the sunny world like a chatterbox, doing its best to be friendly. It bowed to one shore and then to the other so nothing would feel neglected.

By now I could see inside the sunshine and had located my father. He was sitting high on the bank. He wore no hat. Inside the sunlight, his faded red hair was once again ablaze and again in glory. He was reading, although evidently only by sentences because he often looked away from the book. He did not close the book until some time after he saw me.

I scrambled up the bank and asked him, "How many did you get?" He said, "I got all I want." I said, "But how many did you get?" He said. "I got four or five." I asked, "Are they any good?" He said, "They are beautiful."

He was about the only man I ever knew who used the word

"beautiful" as a natural form of speech, and I guess I picked up the habit from hanging around him when I was little.

"How many did you catch?" he asked. "I also caught all I want," I told him. He omitted asking me just how many that was, but he did ask me, "Are they any good?"

"They are beautiful," I told him, and sat down beside him.

"What have you been reading?" I asked. "A book," he said. It was on the ground on the other side of him. So I would not have to bother to look over his knees to see it he said, "A good book."

Then he told me, "In the part I was reading it says the Word was in the beginning, and that's right. I used to think water was first, but if you listen carefully you will hear that the words are underneath the water."

"That's because you are a preacher first and then a fisherman," I told him. "If you ask Paul, he will tell you that the words are formed out of water."

"No," my Father said, "you are not listening carefully. The water runs over the words. Paul will tell you the same thing. Where is Paul anyway?"

I told him he had gone back to fish the first hole over again. "But he promised to be here soon," I assured him. "He'll be here when he catches his limit," he said. "He'll be here, soon," I reassured him, partly because I could already see him in the subterranean shadows.

My father went back to reading and I tried to check what we had said by listening. Paul was fishing fast, picking up one here and there and wasting no time in walking them to shore. When he got directly across from us, he held up a finger on each hand and my father said, "He needs two more for his limit."

I looked to see where the book was left open and knew just enough Greek to recognize Nayos as the Word. I guessed from it and the argument that I was looking at the first verse of John. While I was looking, father said, "He has one on."

It was hard to believe, because he was fishing in front of us on the other side of the hole that father had just fished. Father slowly rose, found a good-sized rock and held it behind his back. Paul landed the fish, and waded out again for number twenty and his limit. Just as he was making the first cast, father threw the rock. He was old enough so that he threw awkwardly and afterward had to rub his shoulder, but the rock landed in the river about where Paul's fly landed and at about the same time, so you can see where my brother learned to throw rocks into his partner's fishing water when he couldn't bear to see his partner catch any more fish.

Paul was startled for only a moment. Then he spotted Father on the bank rubbing his shoulder, and Paul laughed, shook his fist at him, backed to shore and went downstream until he was out of rock range. From there he waded into the water and began to cast again, but now he was far enough away so we couldn't see his line or loops. He was a man with a wand in a river, and whatever happened we had to guess from what the man and the wand and the river did.

As he waded out, his big right arm swung back and forth. Each circle of his arm inflated his chest. Each circle was faster and higher and longer until his arm became defiant and his chest breasted the sky. On shore we were sure, although we could see no line, that the air above him was singing with loops of line that never touched the water but got bigger and bigger each time they passed and sang. And we knew what was in his mind from the lengthening defiance of his arm. He was not going to let his fly touch any water close to shore where the small and middle-sized fish were. We knew from his arm and chest that all parts of him were saying, "No small one for the last one." Everything was going into one big cast for one last big fish.

From our angle high on the bank, my father and I could see where in the distance the wand was going to let the fly first touch water. In the middle of the river was a rock iceberg, just its tip exposed above water and underneath it a rock house. It met all the residential requirements for big fish—powerful water carrying food to the front and back doors, and rest and shade behind them.

My father said, "There has to be a big one out there." I said, "A little one couldn't live out there."

My father said, "The big one wouldn't let it."

My father could tell by the width of Paul's chest that he was going to let the next loop sail. It couldn't get any wider. "I wanted to fish out there," he said, "but I couldn't cast that far."

Paul's body pivoted as if he were going to drive a golf ball three hundred yards, and his arm went high into the great arc and the tip of his wand bent like a spring, and then everything sprang and sang.

Suddenly, there was an end of action. The man was immobile. There was no bend, no power in the wand. It pointed at ten o'clock and ten o'clock pointed at the rock. For a moment the man looked like a teacher with a pointer illustrating something about a rock to a rock. Only water moved. Somewhere above the top of the rock house a fly was swept in water so powerful only a big fish could be there to see it.

Then the universe stepped on its third rail. The wand jumped convulsively as it made contact with the magic current of the world. The wand tried to jump out of the man's right hand. His left hand seemed to be frantically waving goodbye to a fish, but actually was trying to throw enough line into the rod to reduce the voltage and ease the shock of what had struck.

Everything seemed electrically charged but electrically unconnected. Electrical sparks appeared here and there on the river. A fish jumped so far downstream that it seemed outside the man's electrical field, but, when the fish had jumped, the man had leaned back on the rod and it was then that the fish had toppled back into the water not guided in its reentry by itself. The connections between the convulsions and the sparks became clearer by repetition. When the man leaned back on the wand and the fish reentered the water not altogether under its own power, the wand recharged with convulsions, the man's hand waved frantically at another departure, and much farther below a fish jumped again. Because of the connections, it became the same fish.

The fish made three such long runs before another act in the performance began. Although the act involved a big man and a big fish, it looked more like children playing. The man's left hand sneakily began recapturing line, and then, as if caught in the act, threw it all back into the rod as the fish got wise and made still another run.

"He'll get him," I assured my father.

"Beyond doubt," my father said. The line going out became shorter than what the left hand took in.

When Paul peered into the water behind him, we knew he was going to start working the fish to shore and didn't want to back into a hole or rock. We could tell he had worked the fish into shallow water because he held the rod higher and higher to keep the fish from bumping into anything on the bottom. Just when we thought the performance was over, the wand convulsed and the man thrashed through the water after some unseen power departing for the deep.

"The son of a bitch still has fight in him," I thought I said to myself, but unmistakably I said it out loud, and was embarrassed for having said it out loud in front of my father. He said nothing.

Two or three more times Paul worked him close to shore, only to have him swirl and return to the deep, but even at that distance my father and I could feel the ebbing of the underwater power. The rod went high in the air, and the man moved backwards swiftly but evenly, motions which when translated into events meant the fish had tried to rest for a moment on top of the water and the man had quickly raised the rod high and skidded him to shore before the fish thought of getting under water again. He skidded him across the rocks clear back to a sandbar before the shocked fish gasped and discovered he could not live in oxygen. In belated despair, he rose in the sand and consumed the rest of momentary life dancing the Dance of Death on his tail.

The man put the wand down, got on his hands and knees in the sand, and, like an animal, circled another animal and waited. Then the shoulder shot straight out, and my brother stood up, faced us, and, with uplifted arm proclaimed himself the victor. Something giant dangled from his fist. Had Romans been watching they would have thought that what was dangling had a helmet on it.

"That's his limit," I said to my father.

"He is beautiful," my father said, although my brother had just finished catching his limit in the hole my father had already fished.

This was the last fish we were ever to see Paul catch. My father and I talked about this moment several times later, and whatever our other feelings, we always felt it fitting that, when we saw him catch his last fish, we never saw the fish but only the artistry of the fisherman.

While my father was watching my brother, he reached over to pat me, but he missed, so he had to turn his eyes and look for my knee and try again. He must have thought that I felt neglected and that he should tell me he was proud of me also but for other reasons.

It was a little too deep and fast where Paul was trying to wade the river, and he knew it. He was crouched over the water and his arms were spread wide for balance. If you were a wader of big rivers you could have felt with him even at a distance the power of the water making his legs weak and wavy and ready to swim out from under him. He looked downstream to estimate how far it was to an easier place to wade.

My father said, "He won't take the trouble to walk downstream. He'll swim it." At the same time Paul thought the same thing, and put his cigarettes and matches in his hat.

My father and I sat on the bank and laughed at each other. It never occurred to either of us to hurry to the shore in case he needed help with a rod in his right hand and a basket loaded with fish on his left shoulder. In our family it was no great thing for a fisherman to swim a river with matches in his hair. We laughed at each other because we knew he was getting damn good and wet, and we lived in him, and were swept over the rocks with him and held his rod high in one of our hands.

As he moved to shore he caught himself on his feet and then was washed off them, and, when he stood again, more of him showed and he staggered to shore. He never stopped to shake himself. He came charging up the bank showering molecules of water and images of himself to show what was sticking out of his basket, and he dripped all over us, like a young duck dog that in its joy forgets to shake itself before getting close.

"Let's put them all out on the grass and take a picture of them," he said. So we emptied our baskets and arranged them by size and took turns photographing each other admiring them and ourselves. The photographs turned out to be like most amateur snapshots of fishing catches—the fish were white from overexposure and didn't look as big as they actually were and the fishermen looked self-conscious as if some guide had to catch the fish for them.

However, one closeup picture of him at the end of this day remains in my mind, as if fixed by some chemical bath. Usually, just after he finished fishing he had little to say unless he saw he could have fished better. Otherwise, he merely smiled. Now flies danced around his hatband. Large drops of water ran from under his hat on to his face and then into his lips when he smiled.

At the end of this day, then, I remember him both as a distant abstraction in artistry and as a closeup in water and laughter.

My father always felt shy when compelled to praise one of his family, and his family always felt shy when he praised them. My father said, "You are a fine fisherman."

My brother said, "I'm pretty good with a rod, but I need three more years before I can think like a fish,"

Remembering that he had caught his limit by switching to George's No. 2 Yellow Hackle with a feather wing, I said without knowing how much I said. "You already know how to think like a dead stone fly."

We sat on the bank and the river went by. As always, it was making sounds to itself, and now it made sounds to us. It would be hard to find three men sitting side by side who knew better what a river was saying.

Norman Maclean went to Dartmouth College and taught English at the University of Chicago for forty-six years. He started writing A River Runs Through It *after his seventieth birthday. His family finished and published his book* Young Men and Fire, *about the 1949 Mann Gulch fire, in 1992, the same year that Robert Redford directed a film adaptation of* A River Runs Through It *starring Brad Pitt. Maclean died in 1990 at age eighty-seven.*

Fathers Playing Catch With Sons

◆

DONALD HALL

It began with listening to the Brooklyn Dodgers, about 1939, when I was ten years old. The gentle and vivacious voice of Red Barber floated from the Studebaker radio during our Sunday afternoon drives along the shore of Long Island Sound. My mother and my father and I, wedded together in the close front seat, heard the sounds of baseball—and I was tied to those sounds for the rest of my life.

We drove from Connecticut to Ebbets Field, to the Polo Grounds, to Yankee Stadium. When I was at college I went to Fenway Park and to Braves Field. Then, in 1957, I left the East and moved to Michigan. At first, I was cautious about committing myself to the Tigers. The Brooklyn Dodgers had gone to Los Angeles, of all things, and whom could you trust? Al Kaline? Rocky Colavito? Jim Bunning? Norm Cash? I went to Tiger Stadium three or four times a year, and I watched Big Ten college baseball frequently, especially in 1961 when a sophomore football player named Bill Freehan caught for Michigan and, as I remembered, hit .500. The Tigers signed him that summer.

All summer the radio kept going. I wrote letters while I listened to baseball. I might not have known what the score was, but the sound comforted me, a background of distant voices. If rain interrupted the game, I didn't want to hear music; it was baseball radio voices that I wanted to hear.

Baseball is a game of years and of decades. Al Kaline's children grew up. Rocky Colavito was traded, left baseball, became a mushroom farmer, and came back to baseball as a coach. Jim Bunning turned into a great National League pitcher and retired. Norm Cash had a better year at thirty-five than he had had in nearly a decade. And Kaline kept on hitting line drives.

And Jane and I met, and married, and in 1972 the sound of baseball grew louder; Jane loves baseball too. The soft southern sounds of announcers—always from the South, from Red Barber on—filled up the house like plants in the windows, new chairs, and pictures. At night after supper and on weekend afternoons, we heard the long season unwind itself, inning by inning, as vague and precise as ever: the patter of the announcer and, behind him, always, like an artist's calligraphy populating a background more important than the foreground, the baseball sounds of vendors hawking hot dogs, Coke, and programs; the sudden rush of noise from the crowd when a score was posted; the flat slap of a bat and again the swelling crowd yells; the Dixieland between innings; even the beer jingles.

We listened on the dark screen porch, an island in the leaves and bushes, in the faint distant light from the street, while the baseball cricket droned against the real crickets of the yard. We listened while reading newspapers or washing up after dinner. We listened in bed when the Tigers were on the West Coast, just hearing the first innings, then sleeping into the game to wake with the dead gauze sound of the abandoned air straining and crackling beside the bed. Or we went to bed and turned out the lights late in the game, and started to doze as the final pitches gathered in the dark, and when the game ended with a final out and the organ played again, a hand reached out in the dark, over a sleeping shape, to turn off the sound.

And we drove the forty miles to Tiger Stadium, parked on a dingy street in late twilight, and walked to the old green and gray, iron and concrete fort. Tiger Stadium is one of the few old ballparks left, part of the present structure erected in 1912 and the most recent portion in 1938. It is like an old grocer who wears a straw hat and a blue necktie and is frail but don't you ever mention it. It's the old world, Tiger Stadium, as baseball is. It's Hygrade Ball-Park Franks, the smell of fat and mustard, popcorn and spilled beer.

As we approach at night, the sky lights up like a cool dawn. We enter the awkward, homemade-looking, cubist structure, wind through the heavy weaving of its nest, and swing up a dark corridor to the splendid green summer of the field. Balls arch softly from the fungoes, and the fly-shaggers arch them back toward home plate. Batting practice. Infield practice. Pepper. The pitchers loosening up between the dugout and the bullpen. We always get there early. We settle in, breathe quietly the air of baseball, and let the night begin the old rituals again: managers exchange lineups, Tigers take the field, we stand for "our National Anthem," and the batter approaches the plate. . . .

◆　◆　◆

Once I went to an old-timer's game, a few innings of the great players of decades past played before the regular game. The Cincinnati team from 1953—some fifteen members of it—played against a potpourri of retired players from other teams.

The generation of ballplayers slightly older than me, the ballplayers of my childhood and youth, magically returned in their old uniforms and joked and flipped the ball and swung at the slow pitches that the old pitchers lazed up to them. Mickey Vernon played first base, who had played major league ball in the thirties, the forties, the fifties, and the sixties. Carl Erskine pitched. Johnny Mize swung the bat again. Tommy Henrich at fifty-nine stood slim and erect in left field as he had stood for thousands of afternoons in Yankee Stadium. A ball sailed over Gus Bell's head in center field. He plodded after it, his gait heavy and ponderous and painful, while an old catcher dragged himself all the way to third and stood there puffing and gasping. It was grotesque, all of it, like elephants at the circus that waddle and trudge in ballet costumes while the calliope plays Swan Lake.

Yet there was an awkward and frightening beauty to the tableau, as the old men performed stiffly the many motions they had once done nimbly. An old third baseman underhanded the baseball toward the pitcher's mound, as he trotted into the dugout, so that the ball rolled to a stop on the dirt near the rubber; how many thousands of times had he made that gesture in the long summers when he was twenty and thirty?

And Pee Wee Reese played shortstop. I was stunned by Pee Wee because I had known him the longest, from the summer of 1940, when he came up to Brooklyn, until he quit in Los Angeles in 1958. Now he stood at shortstop, again fifty-four years old, leaning all his weight on one slim leg, in a gesture almost effete and certainly graceful.

Suddenly I remembered a scene in grave detail from the beginning of my baseball time. It is a Sunday afternoon, 1940 probably, or possibly 1941, when the Dodgers will win the pennant and meet the Yankees in the series and I will see the first game. My father and my mother and I are riding in the

Studebaker, listening to Red Barber broadcast a crucial game between the Dodgers and the Giants. The Giants are ahead. Now the Dodgers begin to come close—maybe they tie the game; I don't remember the details—and the Giants stop, pause, confer. Then they summon Carl Hubbell from the bullpen.

My father explains how momentous it is that Carl Hubbell should pitch relief. Things have not gone well for him lately. But King Carl is the greatest left-hander of all time, who, in the 1934 All Star game, struck out Babe Ruth, Lou Gehrig, Jimmie Foxx, Al Simmons, and Joe Cronin, all in a row; he's an old screwballer who walks always with his left elbow turned into his ribs, his arm permanently twisted by his best pitch. The great man seldom pitched relief, and now he walked from the bullpen to the pitcher's mound and took his tosses; old man who had pitched since 1928, who couldn't have more than three or four dwindling years left in his arm; old man come in to save the game for his faltering team.

My father's face is tense. He loves the Dodgers and not the Giants, but he loves Carl Hubbell even more. My father is thirty-seven years old in 1940. So is Carl Hubbell.

Then the Dodgers send up a pinch hitter. It is Harold Reese, the baby shortstop, former marbles ("pee-wees") champion of Louisville, Kentucky, fresh from the minor leagues, and fifteen years younger than Hubbell. I sit in the front seat cheering the Dodgers on, hoping against hope, though I realize that the rookie shortstop is "good field no hit."

DONALD HALL

Pee Wee hits a home run off Carl Hubbell and the Dodgers win.

Sitting there in the front seat, eleven years old, I clap and cheer. Then I hear my father's strange voice. I look across my mother to see his knuckles white on the wheel, his face white, and I hear him saying, "The punk! The punk!" With astonishment and horror, I see that my father is crying.

✦ ✦ ✦

My father and I played catch as I grew up. Like so much else between fathers and sons, playing catch was tender and tense at the same time. He wanted to play with me. He wanted me to be good. He seemed to demand that I be good. I threw the ball into his catcher's mitt. Atta boy. Put her right there. I threw straight. Then I tried to put something on it; it flew twenty feet over his head. Or it banged into the sidewalk in front of him, breaking stitches and ricocheting off a pebble into the gutter of Greenway Street. Or it went wide to his right and lost itself in Mrs. Davis's bushes. Or it went wide to his left and rolled across the street while drivers swerved their cars.

I was wild. I was wild. I had to be wild for my father. What else could I be? Would you have wanted me to have control?

But I was, myself, the control on him. He had wanted to teach school, to coach and teach history at Cushing Academy in Ashburnham, Massachusetts, and he had done it for two years before he was married. The salary was minuscule and in the twenties people didn't get married until they had the money to

215

live on. Since he wanted to marry my mother, he made the only decision he could make: he quit Cushing and went into the family business, and he hated business, and he wept when he fired people, and he wept when he was criticized, and his head shook at night, and he coughed from all the cigarettes, and he couldn't sleep, and he almost died when an ulcer hemorrhaged when he was forty-two, and ten years later, at fifty-two, he died of lung cancer.

But the scene I remember happened when he was twenty-five and I was almost one year old. So I do not "remember" it at all. It simply rolls itself before my eyes with the intensity of a lost memory suddenly found again, more intense than the moment itself ever is.

It is 1929, July, a hot Saturday afternoon. At the ballpark near East Rock, in New Haven, Connecticut, just over the Hamden line, my father is playing semipro baseball. I don't know the names of the teams. My mother has brought me in a basket, and she sits under a tree, in the shade, and lets me crawl when I wake up.

My father is very young, very skinny. When he takes off his cap—the uniform is gray, the bill of the cap blue—his fine hair is parted in the middle. His face is very smooth. Though he is twenty-five, he could pass for twenty. He plays shortstop, and he is paid twenty-five dollars a game. I don't know where the money comes from. Do they pass the hat? They would never raise so much money. Do they charge admission? They must charge admission, or I am wrong that it was semipro and that he was paid. Or the whole thing is wrong, a memory I concocted. But of course the reality of 1929—and my mother and the basket and the shade and the heat—does not matter, not to the memory of the living nor to the bones of the dead nor even to the fragmentary images of broken light from that day which wander light-years away in unrecoverable space. What matters is the clear and fine knowledge of this day as it happens now, permanently and repeatedly, on a deep layer of the personal Troy.

There, where this Saturday afternoon of July in 1929 rehearses itself, my slim father performs brilliantly at shortstop. He dives for a low line drive and catches it backhand, somersaults, and stands up holding the ball. Sprinting into left field with his back to the plate, he catches a fly ball that almost drops for a Texas leaguer. He knocks down a ground ball, deep in the hole and nearly to third base, picks it up, and throws the man out at first with a peg as flat as the tape a runner breaks. When he comes up to bat, he feels lucky. The opposing pitcher is a side-armer. He always hits side-armers. So he hits two doubles and a triple, drives in two runs and scores two runs, and his team wins four to three. After the game a man approaches him, while he stands, sweating and tired, with my mother and me in the shade of the elm tree at the rising side of the field.

The man is a baseball scout. He offers my father a contract to play baseball with the Baltimore Orioles, at that time a double-A minor league team. My father is grateful and gratified; he is proud to be offered the job, but he must refuse. After all, he has just started working at the dairy for his father. It wouldn't be possible to leave the job that had been such a decision to take. And besides, he adds, there is the baby.

◆　◆　◆

My father didn't tell me he turned it down because of me. All he told me, or that I think he told me: he was playing semi-pro at twenty-five dollars a game; he had a good day in the field, catching a ball over his shoulder running away from the plate; he had a good day hitting, too, because he could always hit a side-armer. But he turned down the Baltimore Oriole offer. He couldn't leave the dairy then, and besides, he knew that he had just been lucky that day. He wasn't really that good.

But maybe he didn't even tell me that. My mother remembers nothing of this. Or rather she remembers that he played on the team for the dairy, against other businesses, and that she took me to the games when I was a baby. But she remembers nothing of semi-pro, of the afternoon with the side-armer, of the offered contract. Did I make it up? Did my father exaggerate? Men tell stories to their sons, loving and being loved.

I don't care.

Baseball is fathers and sons. Football is brothers beating each other up in the backyard, violent and superficial. Baseball is the generations, looping backward forever with a million apparitions of sticks and balls, cricket and rounders, and the games the Iroquois played in Connecticut before the English came.

Baseball is fathers and sons playing catch, lazy and murderous, wild and controlled, the profound archaic song of birth, growth, age, and death. This diamond encloses what we are.

Donald Hall has published numerous books of poetry, most notably The One Day, *which won the National Book Critics Circle Award, the* Los Angeles Times Book Prize, *and a Pulitzer Prize nomination, and* The Happy Man, *which won the Lenore Marshall Poetry Prize. Hall has also written books on baseball, and published several autobiographical works, including* Life Work *which won the New England Book Award for nonfiction. He has served as poetry editor of* The Paris Review, *and as a member of the editorial board for poetry at Wesleyan University Press. More recently, Hall also served as Poet Laureate of New Hampshire, and in 2006, was appointed the Library of Congress's fourteenth Poet Laureate Consultant in Poetry.*

Tangled Up in Blue

◆

PETER RICHMOND

Nighttime in Los Angeles, on a quiet street off Melrose Avenue. An otherwise normal evening is marked by an oddly whimsical celestial disturbance: Baseballs are falling out of the sky.

They are coming from the roof of a gray apartment building. One ball pocks an adjacent apartment. Another bounces to the street. A third flies off into the night, a mighty shot.

This is West Hollywood in the early eighties, where anything is not only possible but likely—West Hollywood shakes its head and drives on by.

But if a passerby's curiosity had been piqued and he'd climbed to the roof of a neighboring building to divine the source of the show, he would have been rewarded by a most unusual sight: a man of striking looks, with long blond hair, startlingly and wincingly thin, hitting the ball with a practiced swing—a flat, smooth, even stroke developed during a youth spent in minor-league towns from Pocatello to Albuquerque.

This is not Tommy Lasorda Jr.'s routine nighttime activity. A routine night is spent in the clubs, the bright ones and dark ones alike.

Still, on occasion, here he'd be, on the roof, clubbing baseballs into the night. Because there were times when the pull was just too strong. Of the game. Of the father. He could never be what his father was—Tommy Lasorda's own inner orientation made that impossible—but he could fantasize, couldn't he? That he was ten, taking batting practice in Ogden, Utah, with his dad, and Garvey, and the rest of them?

And so, on the odd night, on a night he was not at Rage, or the Rose Tattoo, he'd climb to the roof, the lord of well-tanned West Hollywood, and lose himself in the steady rhythm of bat hitting ball—the reflex ritual that only a man inside the game can truly appreciate.

"Junior was the better hitter," recalls Steve Garvey. "He didn't have his father's curveball, but he was the better hitter."

"I cried," Tom Lasorda says quietly. He is sipping a glass of juice in the well-appointed lounge of Dodgertown, the Los Angeles baseball team's green-glorious oasis of a spring-training site. It's a place that heralds and nurtures out-of-time baseball and out-of-time Dodgers. A place where, each spring, in the season of illusion's renewal, they are allowed to be the men they once were.

On this February weekend, Dodgertown is crowded with clearly affluent, often out-of-shape white men, each of whom has parted with $4,000 to come to Dodgers fantasy camp. In pink polo shirts and pale-pink slacks—the pastels of privilege—they are scattered around the lounge, flirting with fantasy lives, chatting with the coaches.

"I cried. A lot of times. But I didn't cry in the clubhouse. I kept my problems to myself. I never brought them with me. I didn't want to show my family—that's my family away from my house. What's the sense of bringing my problems to my team?

"I had him for thirty-three years. Thirty-three years is better than nothing, isn't it? If I coulda seen God and God said to me 'I'm going to give you a son for thirty-three years and take him away after thirty-three years,' I'd have said 'Give him to me.'"

His gaze skips about the room—he always seems to be looking around for someone to greet, a hand to shake, another camper to slap another anecdote on. Tom Lasorda floats on an ever-flowing current of conversation.

"I signed that contract [to manage the Dodgers] with a commitment to do the best of my ability," he says. "If I'm depressed, what good does it do? When I walk into the clubhouse, I got to put on a winning face. A happy face. If I go in with my head hung down when I put on my uniform, what good does it do?"

These are words he has said before, in response to other inquiries about Tommy's death. But now the voice shifts tone and the words become more weighted; he frames each one with a new meaning.

And he stops looking around the room and looks me in the eye.

"I could say 'God. why was I dealt this blow? Does my wife—do I—deserve this? [But] then how do I feel, hunh? Does it change it?" Now the voice grows even louder, and a few fantasy campers raise their eyebrows and turn their heads toward us.

"See my point?"

The words are like fingers jabbed into my chest.

"Hunh?"

Then his eyes look away and he sets his face in a flat, angry look of defiance.

"You could hit me over the head with a fucking two-by-four and you don't knock a tear out of me," he says.

"Fuck," he says.

The word does not seem to be connected to anything.

He was the second of five sons born, in Norristown, Pennsylvania, a crowded little city-town a half-hour north of Philadelphia, to Sabatino Lasorda, a truck driver who'd emigrated from Italy, and Carmella Lasorda.

By the age of twenty-two, Tom Lasorda was a successful minor league pitcher by trade, a left-hander with a curveball and not a lot more. But he was distinguished by an insanely dogged belief in the possibility of things working out. His father had taught him that. On winter nights when he could not turn the heat on, Sabatino Lasorda would nonetheless present an unfailingly optimistic face to his family, and that was how Tom Lasorda learned that nothing could stomp on the human spirit if you didn't let it.

Tom Lasorda played for teams at nearly every level of professional ball: in Concord, New Hampshire; Schenectady, New York; Greenville, South Carolina; Montreal; Brooklyn (twice, briefly); Kansas City, Missouri; Denver; and Los Angeles. Once, after a short stay in Brooklyn, he was sent back to the minors so the Dodgers could keep a left-handed pitcher with a good fastball named Sandy Koufax, and to this day Lasorda will look you in the eye and say "I still think they made a mistake" and believe it.

The Dodgers saw the white-hot burn and made it into a minor-league manager. From 1965 to 1972, Lasorda's teams—in Pocatello, Ogden, Spokane, then Albuquerque—finished second, first, first, first, second, first, third and first. Sheer bravado was the tool; tent-preaching thick with obscenities the style.

In 1973, the Dodgers called him to coach for the big team, and he summoned his wife and his son and his daughter from Norristown, and they moved to Fullerton, California, a feature-less sprawl of a suburb known for the homogeneity of its style of life and the conservatism of its residents.

In 1976, he was anointed the second manager in the Los Angeles Dodgers' nineteen-year history. His managing style was by instinct, not by the book, and his instincts were good enough to pay off more often than not. In his first two years, the Dodgers made the World Series. In 1981, they won it. In 1985, they didn't make it because Lasorda elected to have Tom Niedenfuer pitch to St. Louis's Jack Clark in the sixth game of the playoffs, against the odds, and Jack Clark hit a three-run home run. In 1988, though, he sent a limping Kirk Gibson to the plate and gave us a moment for history.

From the first, Lasorda understood that he had to invent a new identity for this team, the team that Walter O'Malley had yanked out of blue-collar-loyal Brooklyn-borough America and dropped into a city whose only real industry was manufacturing the soulless stuff of celluloid fantasy. His clubhouse became a haunt for show-business personalities, usually of distinctly out-sized demeanor—Sinatra, Rickles—and he himself became the beacon of a new mythology, leader of the team that played in a ballpark on a hill on a road called Elysian, perched above the downtown, high and imperious. Because, really, aren't there too many theme parks to compete with in Los Angeles to manage your baseball team as anything other than another one?

In sixteen years, the tone of the sermon has seldom faltered, at least not before this year. This year, through no fault of Tom Lasorda's, his fielders have forgotten how to field, in a game in which defense has to be an immutable; and if this is anyone's fault, it's that of the men who stock the farm system. His pitching is vague, at best. So the overwhelming number of one-run games— most of which the Dodgers lost—is, in fact, testament, again, to Lasorda's management. No one has questioned his competence.

His spirit has flagged considerably, but his days, in season and out, are as full of Dodger Blue banquet appearances as ever, with impromptu Dodgers pep rallies in airport concourses from Nashville to Seattle. Unlike practitioners of Crystal Cathedral pulpitry, Lasorda the tent-preacher believes in what he says, which, of course, makes all the difference in the world. Because of his faith, Dodger Blue achieves things, more things than you can imagine. The lights for the baseball field in Caledonia, Mississippi; the fund for the former major leaguer with cancer in Pensacola: Tom showed up, talked Dodger Blue, raised the money. Tom's word maintains the baseball field at Jackson State and upgraded the facilities at Georgia Tech.

"I was in Nashville," Tom says, still sitting in the lounge, back on automatic now, reciting. "Talking to college baseball coaches, and a buddy told me nine nuns had been evicted from their home. I got seven or eight dozen balls [signed by Hall of Fame players], we auctioned them, and we built them a home. They said, 'We prayed for a miracle, and God sent you to us.'"

Nine nuns in Nashville.

In the hallway between the lounge and the locker room hang photographs of Brooklyn Dodgers games. Lasorda has pored over them a thousand times, with a thousand writers, a thousand campers, a thousand Dodgers prospects—identifying each player, re-creating each smoky moment.

But on this day, a few minutes after he's been talking about Tommy, he walks this gauntlet differently.

"That's Pete Reiser," Tom Lasorda says. "He's dead." He points to another player. He says, "He's dead." He walks down the hallway, clicking them off, talking out loud but to himself.

"He's dead. He's dead. He's dead. He's dead. He's dead."

Back in his suite, in the residence area of Dodgertown, I ask him if it was difficult having a gay son.

"My son wasn't gay," he says evenly, no anger. "No way. No way. I read that in a paper. I also read in that paper that a lady gave birth to a fuckin' monkey, too. That's not the fuckin' truth. That's not the truth."

I ask him if he read in the same paper that his son had died of AIDS.

"That's not true," he says.

I say that I thought a step forward had been taken by Magic

Johnson's disclosure of his own HIV infection, that that's why some people in Los Angeles expected him to . . .

"Hey," he says. "I don't care what people . . . I know what my son died of. I know what he died of. The doctor put out a report of how he died. He died of pneumonia."

He turns away and starts to brush his hair in the mirror of his dressing room. He is getting ready to go to the fantasy-camp barbecue. He starts to whistle. I ask him if he watched the ceremony on television when the Lakers retired Johnson's number.

"I guarantee you one fuckin' thing," he says. "I'll lay you three to one Magic plays again [in the NBA]. Three to one. That Magic plays again."

As long as he's healthy, I say. People have lived for ten years with the right medication and some luck. Your quality of life can be good, I say.

Lasorda doesn't answer. Then he says, "You think people would have cared so much if it had been Mike Tyson?"

On death certificates issued by the state of California, there are three lines to list the deceased's cause of death, and after each is a space labeled TIME INTERVAL BETWEEN ONSET AND DEATH.

Tom Lasorda Jr.'s death certificate reads:

IMMEDIATE CAUSE: A) PNEUMONITIS—2 WEEKS
DUE TO: B) DEHYDRATION—6 WEEKS

DUE TO: C) PROBABLE ACQUIRED IMMUNO DEFICIENCY
SYNDROME—1 YEAR

At Sunny Hills High School, in Fullerton, California—"the most horrible nouveau riche white-bread high school in the world," recalls Cat Gwynn, a Los Angeles photographer and filmmaker and a Sunny Hills alumna—Tommy Lasorda moved through the hallways with a style and a self-assurance uncommon in a man so young; you could see them from afar, Tommy and his group. They were all girls, and they were all very pretty. Tommy was invariably dressed impeccably. He was as beautiful as his friends. He had none of his father's basset-hound features; Tommy's bones were carved, gently, from glass.

"It was very obvious that he was feminine, but none of the jocks nailed him to the wall or anything," Gwynn says. "I was enamored of him because he wasn't at all uncomfortable with who he was. In this judgmental, narrow-minded high school, he strutted his stuff."

In 1980, at the Fashion Institute of Design and Merchandising, Cindy Stevens and Tommy Lasorda shared a class in color theory. Tommy, Stevens recalls, often did not do his homework. He would spend a lot of his time at Dodgers games or on the road with the team. At school, they shared cigarettes in the hallway. Tommy would tell her about the latest material he'd bought to have made into a suit. She'd ask him where the money came from. Home, he'd say.

"He talked lovingly about his father and their relationship—they had a very good relationship," Stevens says now. "I was surprised. I didn't think it'd be like that. You'd think it'd be hard on a macho Italian man. This famous American idol. You'd figure it'd be [the father saying] 'Please don't let people know you're my son,' but it was the opposite. I had new respect for his father. There had to be acceptance from his mom and dad. Tommy had that good self-esteem—where you figure that [his] parents did something right."

In the late seventies, Tommy left Fullerton, moving only an hour northwest in distance—though he might as well have been crossing the border between two sovereign nations—to West Hollywood, a pocket of gay America unlike any other, a community bound by the shared knowledge that those within it had been drawn by its double distinction: to be among gays, and to be in Hollywood. And an outrageous kid from Fullerton, ready to take the world by storm, found himself dropped smack into the soup—of a thousand other outrageous kids, from Appleton, and Omaha, and Scranton.

But Tommy could never stand to be just another anything. The father and the son had that in common. They had a great deal in common. Start with the voice: gravelly, like a car trying to start on a cold morning. The father, of course, spends his life barking and regaling, never stopping; he's baseball's oral poet, an anti-Homer. It's a well-worn voice. Issuing from the son, a man so attractive that men tended to assume he was a woman, it was the most jarring of notes. One of his closest friends compared it to Linda Blair's in *The Exorcist*—the scenes in which she was possessed.

More significantly, the father's world was no less eccentric than the son's: The subset of baseball America found in locker rooms and banquet halls is filled with men who have, in large part, managed quite nicely to avoid the socialization processes of the rest of society.

Then, the most obvious similarity: Both men were so outrageous, so outsized and surreal in their chosen persona, that, when it came down to it, for all of one's skepticism about their sincerity, it was impossible not to like them—not to, finally, just give in and let their version of things wash over you, rather than resist. Both strutted an impossibly simplistic view of the world— the father with his gospel of fierce optimism and blind obeisance to a baseball mythology, and the son with a slavery to fashion that he carried to the point of religion.

But where the illusion left off and reality started, that was a place hidden to everyone but themselves. In trying to figure out what each had tucked down deep, we can only conjecture. "You'd be surprised what agonies people have," Dusty Baker, the former Dodger, reminds us, himself a good friend of both father and son, a solid citizen in a sport that could use a few more. "There's that old saying that we all have something that's hurting us."

In the case of the son, friends say the West Hollywood years were born of a *Catch-22* kind of loneliness: The more bizarre the lengths to which he went to hone the illusion, the less accessible he became. In his last years, friends say, everything quieted down, markedly so. The flamboyant life gave way to a routine of health clubs and abstinence and sobriety and religion. But by then, of course, the excesses of the earlier years had taken their inexorable toll.

As for the father, there's no question about the nature of the demon he's been prey to for the past two years. Few in his locker room saw any evidence of sadness as his son's illness grew worse, but this should come as no surprise: Tom Lasorda has spent most of four decades in the same baseball uniform. Where else would he go to get away from the grief?

"Maybe," Baker says, "his ballpark was his sanctuary."

It's a plague town now, there's no way around it. At brunch at the French Quarter, men stop their conversations to lay out their pills on the tables, and take them one by one with sips of juice. A mile west is Rage, its name having taken on a new meaning. Two blocks away, on Santa Monica Boulevard, at A Different Light, atop the shelves given over to books on how to manage to stay alive for another few weeks, sit a dozen clear bottles, each filled with amber fluid and a rag—symbolic Molotovs, labeled with the name of a man or a woman or a government agency that is setting back the common cause, reinforcing the stereotypes, driving the social stigmata even deeper into West Hollywood's already weakened flesh.

But in the late seventies, it was a raucous, outrageous and

joyous neighborhood, free of the pall that afflicted hetero Los Angeles, thronged as it was with people who'd lemminged their way out west until there was no more land, fugitives from back east.

In the late seventies and the early eighties, say his friends and his acquaintances and those who knew him and those who watched him, Tommy Lasorda was impossible to miss. They tell stories that careen from wild and touching to sordid and scary; some ring true, others fanciful. Collected, they paint a neon scar of a boy slashing across the town. They trace the path of a perfect, practiced, very lonely shooting star.

His haunt was the Rose Tattoo, a gay club with male strippers, long closed now. One night, he entered—no, he made an entrance—in a cape, with a pre-power ponytail and a cigarette holder: Garbo with a touch of Bowie and the sidelong glance of Veronica Lake. He caught the eye of an older man. They talked. In time, became friends. In the early eighties, they spent a lot of time together. Friends is all they were. They were very much alike.

"I'm one of those gentlemen who liked him," says the man. "I was his Oscar Wilde. He liked me because I was an older guy who'd tasted life. I was his Mame. I showed him life. Art. Theater. I made him a little more sophisticated. [Showed him] how to dress a little better."

They spent the days poolside at a private home up behind the perfect pink stucco of the Beverly Hills Hotel, Tommy lacquering himself with a tan that was the stuff of legend. The tan is de rigueur. The tan is all. It may not look like work, but it is; the work is to look as good as you can.

He occasionally held a job, never for long. Once, he got work at the Right Bank, a shoe store, to get discounts. His father bought him an antique-clothing store. He wearied of it. Tommy, says one friend, wanted to be like those women in soap operas who have their own businesses but never actually work at them.

Tommy's look was his work. If there were others who were young and lithe and handsome and androgynous, none were as outré as Tommy. Tommy never ate. A few sprouts, some fruit, a potato. Tommy spent hours at the makeup table. Tommy studied portraits of Dietrich and Garbo to see how the makeup was done. Tommy bleached his hair. On his head. On his legs. Tommy had all of his teeth capped. Tommy had a chemabrasion performed on his face, in which an acid bath removes four of the skin's six layers. Then the skin is scrubbed to remove yet another layer. It is generally used to erase scars or wrinkles. Tommy had two done.

But he smoked, and he drank. Champagne in a flute, cigarette in a long holder, graceful and vampish at the same time: This was Tommy at the Rose Tattoo. His friend also remembers how well Tommy and his father got along. His friend would drive Tommy to the Italian restaurant where he'd meet his father for Sunday dinners.

"He loved his father, you know. They got along perfectly

well," His friend was never his lover. Only his friend. That was all. That was enough. "He was very lonely."

On occasion, the nighttime ramble led him far from the stilted elegance of Santa Monica Boulevard. In the punk clubs, amid the slam-dancing and the head-butting, Tommy parted the leathered seas, a chic foil for all the pierced flesh and fury, this man who didn't sweat. This man who crossed himself when someone swore in public.

Penelope Spheeris met him at Club Zero. She would go on to direct the punk documentary *The Decline of Western Civilization* and, years later, *Wayne's World*. They became friends. They met at punk clubs—the blond man in custom-made suits, the striking woman in black cocktail dresses and leather boots. In 1981, she interviewed Tommy for a short-lived underground paper called *No Mag*.

> PENELOPE: Have you been interviewed very much before?
> TOMMY: No, but I'm very . . . *oral* . . .
> PENELOPE: People who would see you around town, they would probably think, you were gay.
> TOMMY: *I don't care.*
> PENELOPE: What do you do when you get that reaction from them?
> TOMMY: I like all people. And it's better having comments, be it good, bad or whatever. I don't mind at all, but I

dress quite ... well, I wouldn't say it's flamboyant because it's not intentional. *It's just intentionally me.*

PENELOPE: O.K., but you understand, when somebody looks at a picture of you, they're going to say, *this guy's awfully feminine.*

TOMMY: I'm there for anyone to draw any conclusions.

PENELOPE: Are you?

TOMMY: Well, I mean, I've done different things ... of course. I have *no label on myself* because then I have restrictions. I would really hate to state anything like that.

PENELOPE: When you were young did your dad say, "Come on, Tommy, Jr., *let's go play baseball*"?

TOMMY: *Never.* They always allowed me to do exactly what I pleased. I don't know how they had the sense to be that way. As parents they're both so ... well, very straight-laced and conservative. I don't know how I was allowed to just be me, but I think it was because I was so strongly me that I don't think they thought they could ever stop it ....

PENELOPE: Do you feel like you should be careful in the public eye?

TOMMY: *I feel like I should,* but I don't.

PENELOPE: Do you think the press would be mean to you if they had the chance?

TOMMY: I'm sure they would, but I'll take any publicity.

PENELOPE: Why?

TOMMY: Because that's what I want ... I do everything to
be seen.

"I found him totally fascinating. He was astoundingly beautiful, more than most women," Spheeris says now. "I became
interested in ... the blatant contrast in lifestyles. Tommy Lasorda
Sr. was so involved in that macho sports world, and his son was
the opposite ..."

She laughs.

"I was astounded at how many clothes he had. I remember
walking into the closet. The closet was as big as my living room.
Everything was organized perfectly. Beautiful designer clothes
he looked great in."

Often in the early eighties, when fashion photographer
Eugene Pinkowski's phone would ring, it would be Tommy.
Tommy wanting to shop or Tommy wanting Eugene to photo-
graph his new look.

When they went shopping, they would fly down Melrose in
Tommy's Datsun 280Z, much, much too fast, Tommy leaning
out of the driver's window, hair flying in the wind, like some
Valley Girl gone weird, hurling gravelly insults ("Who did your
hair? It looks awful.") at the pedestrians diving out of the way.

He was a terrible driver. Once he hit a cat. He got out of the
car, knelt on the street and cried. He rang doorbells up and down
the street, trying to find the owner.

Tommy would call to tell Eugene he was going to buy him a gift. Then Tommy would spend all his money on himself. Then, the next day. Tommy would make up for it. He would hand him something. A pair of porcelain figures, babies, a boy and a girl, meant to be displayed on a grand piano—very difficult to find, very expensive.

Then the phone would ring. It'd be Eugene's mother, saying she just got a bracelet. From his friend Tommy.

"He was a character," Pinkowski says at breakfast in a Pasadena coffee shop. "He was a case. He was a complete and total case."

Then he looks away.

"He was really lonely," Pinkowski says. "He was sad."

When he was being photographed, Tommy was always trying to become different people.

Eugene captured them all. Tommy with long hair. With short hair. With the cigarette. Without it. With some of his exceptionally beautiful women friends. Tommy often had beautiful women around him, Pinkowski recalls—vaguely European, vaguely models. Sometimes Tommy had Pinkowski take pictures of them.

Mostly he took pictures of Tommy. Tommy with a stuffed fox. Lounging on the floor. In the piano. Sitting in a grocery cart.

In red. In green. In white. In blue. In black and gray.

His four toes. Tommy had four toes on his right foot, the

fifth lost in a childhood accident. He posed the foot next to a gray boot on the gray carpet. Then he posed it next to a red shoe on the gray carpet. The red looked better.

Tommy and his foot were a regular subject of conversation, often led by Tommy.

"Tommy was a great storyteller, and he'd tell you stories of his dad in the minor leagues," Pinkowski says. "Everybody'd like him. He was very much like the old boy. He could really hold his own in a group of strangers. And he'd do anything to keep it going. To be the center of attention. He'd just suddenly take his shoe and sock off at dinner and say 'Did you know I was missing my toe?'"

One day, Tommy wanted to pose wrapped in a transparent shower curtain. Tommy was wearing white underwear. For forty-five minutes they tried to light the shot so that the underwear was concealed, to no avail. Tommy left, and returned in flesh-colored underwear.

There was nothing sexual about Tommy's fashion-posing. Tommy's fashion-posing was designed to get Tommy into fashion magazines. Tommy was forever bugging the editors of *Interview* to feature him, but they wouldn't.

"As beautiful as he was, as famous as his father was, he thought he should be in magazines," Pinkowski says now. "He was as hungry as Madonna. But Bowie and Grace [Jones] could do something. He couldn't do anything. He could never see any talent in himself."

The closest Tommy came was when he bought himself a full

page in *Stuff* magazine, in 1982, for a picture of himself that Eugene took.

He would pay Eugene out of the house account his parents had set up for him. On occasion, Eugene would get a call from Tommy's mother: We don't need any more pictures this year. Still, Tommy would have several of his favorites printed for his parents. One is from the blue period.

At the Duck Club, down behind the Whiskey, in 1985, Tommy sat in a corner drinking Blue Hawaiians. To match his blue waistcoat. Or his tailored blue Edwardian gabardine jacket. This was during his blue period. In his green period, he was known to wear a green lamé wrap and drink crème de menthe. But the blue period lasted longer. The good thing about the blue period was that on the nights he didn't want to dress up, he could wear denim and still match his drink. And, sometimes, his mood.

"He walked around with a big smile on his face, as if everything was great because he had everything around him to prove it was great," Spheeris says. "But I don't think it was . . . When you're that sad, you have to cover up a lot of pain. But he didn't admit it."

The nature of the pain will forever be in debate. Few of his friends think it had to do with the relationship with his parents.

"The parents—both of them—were incredibly gracious and kind to everyone in Tommy's life," says a close friend of the family's.

Alex Magno was an instructor at the Voight Fitness and Dance Center and became one of Tommy's best friends. Tommy was the godfather of his daughter. "We used to ask him 'You're thirty-three, what kind of life is that—you have no responsibilities. Why don't you work?'" says Magno. "You lose your identity when you don't have to earn money, you know what I mean? Everything he owns, his parents gave him. I never heard him say, 'I want to do my own thing.' When you get used to the easy life, it's hard to go out there. I don't think he appreciated what he had."

He loved the Dodgers. He attended many games each season. His father regularly called him from the road. In his office at Dodger Stadium, the father kept a photograph of Tommy on his desk.

Tommy loved the world of the Dodgers. He loved the players. To friends who were curious about his relationship with his father's team—and all of them were—he said it was great. He told Spheeris they were a turn-on.

"He was a good, sensitive kid," says Dusty Baker, now a coach with the San Francisco Giants. "There was an article one time. Tommy said I was his favorite player because we used to talk music all the time. He loved black female artists. He turned me on to Linda Clifford. He loved Diana Ross. He loved Thelma Houston.

"Some of the guys kidded me. Not for long. Some of the guys would say stuff—you know how guys are—but most were pretty cool. That's America. Everybody's not going to be cool.

Most people aren't going to be. Until they have someone close to them afflicted. Which I have."

Baker spent last Christmas Eve distributing turkey dinners with the Shanti Foundation, an AIDS-education group in California.

"There are a lot of opinions about Tom Junior, about how [his father] handled his relationship with his son," says Steve Garvey, who more than anyone was the onfield embodiment of Dodger Blue. "Everyone should know that there is this Tom [senior] who really loved his son and was always there for him. The two loving parents tried to do as much for him as he chose to let them do . . . Junior chose a path in life, and that's his prerogative. That's every individual's right."

Garvey attended the memorial service for Alan Wiggins, his former teammate on the San Diego Padres, who died of an AIDS-related illness last year, after a seven-year career in the majors.

"He was a teammate, we always got along well, he gave me one hundred percent effort, played right next to me. I think the least you can do, when you go out and play in front of a million people and sweat and pull muscles and bleed and do that as a living, when that person passes away, is be there. It's the right thing to do."

Garvey was the only major league baseball player at Wiggins's service. I ask him if he was surprised that he was alone.

"Not too much surprises me in life anymore," Garvey says.

In the mid-1980s, Tommy's style of life changed. It may have been because he learned that he had contracted the human immunodeficiency virus. According to Alex Magno, he knew he was infected for years before his death. It may have been that he simply grew weary of the scene, it may have been that he grew up.

He entered a rehabilitation program. He became a regular at the Voight gym, attending classes seven days a week. Henry Siegel, the Voight's proprietor, was impressed by Tommy's self-assurance and generosity. Tommy moved out of his West Hollywood place into a new condo in Santa Monica, on a quiet, neat street a few blocks from the beach—an avenue of trimmed lawns and stunning gardens displayed beneath the emerald canopies of old and stalwart trees. "T. L. JR." reads the directory outside the locked gate; beyond it, a half-dozen doorways open onto a carefully tiled courtyard. The complex also features Brooke Shields on its list of tenants.

He was a quiet tenant, a thoroughly pleasant man. He had a new set of friends—whom he regaled, in his best raconteurial fashion, with tales of the past.

"Tommy used to tell us incredible stuff about how he used to be . . . everything he'd done—drugs, sleeping with women, sleeping with men," says Magno.

"He went through the homosexual thing and came out of it," Magno continues. "Gay was the thing to be back when he first came to L.A. Tommy used to tell his friends he had been gay. He didn't pretend. He let people know he had been this wild, crazy guy who had changed. He was cool in that. When you got to meet him, you got to know everything about him."

Including that he slept with guys?

"Yes. But . . . he didn't want to admit he had AIDS because people would say he was gay."

This apparent contradiction surfaces regularly in the tale of Tommy Lasorda.

"I think he wanted to make his father happy," says his Oscar Wilde. "But he didn't know how to. He wanted to be more macho but didn't know how to. He wanted to please his dad. He wished he could have liked girls. He tried."

No one who knew Tommy in the seventies and the early eighties recalls him having a steady romantic relationship. Pinkowski remarks on the asexual nature of the masks his friend kept donning—and about how his friend kept some sides of himself closed off. "He'd never talk about being gay. He'd never reveal himself that way. He'd never say anything about anybody that way."

"Of course he was gay," says Jeff Kleinman, the manager of a downtown restaurant who used to travel the same club circuit as Lasorda in the early eighties. "No, I never saw him with another guy as a couple. [But] just because a man doesn't have a date doesn't mean he isn't gay! To say he wasn't gay would be like saying Quentin Crisp isn't gay. How could you hide a butterfly that was so beautiful?"

"Please," says his Oscar Wilde. "He was gay. He was gay. He was gay."

"Gay," of course, is not a word that describes sexual habits. It speaks of a way of living. No one interviewed for this story thought that Tommy wasn't gay; reactions to his father's denial range from outrage and incredulity to laughter and a shake of the head. Former major league umpire Dave Pallone, who revealed his own homosexuality in an autobiography two years ago, knows the father well, and also knew his son.

"Tommy Sr. is, as far as I'm concerned, a tremendous man," says Pallone. "I consider him a friend. I have a lot of empathy for what he's going through. [But] as far as I'm concerned, I don't think he ever accepted the fact that his son was a gay man. I knew him to be a gay man, and I knew a lot of people who knew him as a gay man.

"We don't want to be sexual beings. We just want to be human beings."

"If nothing else, his father should be proud that he repented," Alex Magno says. "He'd come a long way—denying what he used to be, so happy with what he'd become."

I tell him his father denies the illness.

"He died of AIDS," Magno says. "There's no question. But what difference does it make? He was a good man. He was a great man. You shouldn't judge. He had had no sex for a long time. We didn't know how he could do that. I mean . . . but he was incredible. He gave up everything. That's what he said, and there was no reason not to believe him. He was totally like a normal man. He was still feminine—that gets in your system—but there was no lust after men."

In the last two years of his life, Tommy's illness took its toll on his looks. He was not ashamed, though. The surface self-assurance remained. One night, he made an entrance into Rage—thinner, not the old Tommy, but acting every bit the part. He still showed up at Dodger Stadium, too, with his companion, a woman named Cathy Smith, whom Tom senior said was Tommy's fiancée. When he did, he was as elegant and debonair as ever: wide-brimmed hats, tailored suits.

"Nobody in their right mind is going to say it's not difficult— I know how difficult it is for them to try and understand their son," Dave Pallone says. "And to accept the fact he's not with them and what the real reason is. But . . . here was a chance wasted. The way you get rid of a fear is by attacking it . . . . Can you imagine if the Dodgers, who are somewhat conservative, could stand up and say 'We understand this is a problem that needs to be addressed . . . We broke down the barriers from the beginning with Jackie Robinson. Why can't we break down the barriers with the AIDS epidemic?'"

A close friend who was with Tommy the day before his death vehemently disagrees.

"If his father has to accept his son's death right now in that way, let him do it," she says. "If he can't accept things yet, he may never be able to . . . but what good does it do? [Tom's] world is a different world. We should all do things to help, yes, but at the same time, this is a child who someone's lost. Some people have the fortitude, but they simply don't have the strength . . . . There comes a point, no matter how public they may be, [at which] we need to step back and let them be. You can't force people to face what they don't want to face without hurting them."

"There's something wrong with hiding the truth," Penelope Spheeris says. "It's just misplaced values. It is a major denial. People need to know these things. Let's get our values in the right place. That's all."

"I'm in a position where I can help people, so I help people," Tom Lasorda says. We are strolling through the night in Dodgertown, toward the fantasy-camp barbecue. "You don't realize the enjoyment I got with those nuns in that convent. I can't describe how good that made me feel."

I ask him what his dad would say if he were alive.

"I think he'd have been so proud of me. My father was the greatest man."

He tells me that his winters are so busy with appearances that "you wouldn't believe it." I ask him why he doesn't slow down.

"I don't know," he says. "I like to help people. I like to give something back."

On Valentine's Day, 1991, Eugene Pinkowski's phone rang. It was Tommy. His voice was weak.

"He was typical Tommy. He was really noble about it. He was weak, you could tell. I was so sad. He said, in that voice, 'I'm sure you've read that I'm dying. Well, I am.'

"Then he said, 'Thank you for being so nice to me during my lifetime.' He said, 'I want to thank you, because you made me look good.'"

On June 3, 1991, with his parents and his sisters at his bedside, in the apartment on the cool, flower-strewn street, Tommy Lasorda died.

His memorial service was attended by Frank Sinatra and Don Rickles. Pia Zadora sang "The Way We Were," one of Tommy junior's favorite songs.

Tom Lasorda asked that all donations go to the Association of Professional Ball Players of America, a charity that helps former ballplayers in need, one of two charities to which baseball players in trouble can turn for help. It is a conservative group, known for its refusal to offer assistance to ballplayers who fall into the trap of substance abuse.

In the coffee shop in Pasadena, it is late morning, and Eugene Pinkowski is lingering, remembering. His Tommy portfolio is spread across the table. Tommy is smiling at us from a hundred pictures.

I ask Eugene if Tommy would have wanted this story written.

"Are you kidding?" he says. "If there's any sort of afterlife. Tommy is looking down and cheering. This is something he wanted. To be remembered like this. He'd be in heaven."

Peter Richmond is an award-winning reporter and was a feature writer for GQ *magazine for two decades. He has covered everything from Rosemary Clooney to sports, and his work has also appeared in* The New Yorker, Vanity Fair, The New York Times Magazine, *and* Rolling Stone. *He has appeared many times on National Public Radio's* Morning Edition. *He lives in Dutchess County, New York.*

Friday Night Lights

◆

BUZZ BISSINGER

hen his father gazed at him from the hospital bed with those sad eyes that had drawn so narrow from the drinking and the smoking and the endless heartache, Mike Winchell had been thirteen years old. He knew something was wrong because of the way his father acted with him, peaceful in the knowledge he didn't have to put up a fight anymore. Mike tried to joke with him as he always had, but Billy Winchell didn't have time for playful banter. He was serious now, and he wanted Mike to listen.

He brought up Little League and warned Mike that the pitchers were going to get better now and the home runs would not come as easily as they once had. He told him he had to go to college, there could be no two ways about it. He let him know it was okay to have a little beer every now and then because the Winchells were, after all, German, and Germans loved their beer, but he admonished him to never, ever try drugs. And he told his son he loved him.

He didn't say much more after that, the arthritis eating into his hips and the agony of the oil field accident that had cost him his leg too much for him now. In the late night silence of that hospital room in Odessa, he let go.

Mike ran out of the room when it happened, wanting to be by himself, to get as far away as he possibly could, and his older brother, Joe Bill, made no attempt to stop him. He knew Mike would be back because he had always been that kind of kid, quiet, loyal, unfailingly steady. Mike didn't go very far. He stopped in front of the fountain at the hospital entrance and sat by himself. It was one in the morning and hardly anything stirred in those wide downtown streets. He cried a little but he knew he would be all right because, ever since the split-up of his parents when he was five, he had pretty much raised himself. Typically, he didn't worry about himself. He worried about his grandmother.

But he didn't want to stay in Odessa anymore. It was too ugly for him and the land itself bore no secrets nor ever inspired the imagination, so damn flat, as he later put it, that a car ran down the highway and never disappeared. He longed for lakes and trees and hills, for serene places where he could take walks by himself.

Mike came back to the hospital after about half an hour. "You were the most special thing in his life," his brother told him. "It's a hard pill to swallow, but you're gonna have to make him proud of you." As for leaving Odessa to come live with him, Joe Bill gently talked Mike out of it. He used the most powerful pull there was for a thirteen-year-old boy living in Odessa, really the only one that gave a kid something to dream about—the power of Permian football.

He talked about how Mike had always wanted to wear the black and white and how much he would regret it if he didn't because there were so few places that could offer the same sense of allegiance and tradition. Mike knew that Joe Bill was right. He had already carried that dream for a long time, and despite what he thought of Odessa, it was impossible to let it go.

He stayed in Odessa and sometimes, when he went over to his grandmother's house and talked about his father, it helped him through the pain of knowing that Billy was gone forever. "His daddy worshiped him," said Julia Winchell. "He sure loved that little boy." And Mike returned that love.

"When he died, I just thought that the best person in the world had just died."

Billy and Mike.

There was Mike, smiling, curly-haired, looking into his dad's face at Christmastime. And there was Billy, thin and wizened and slightly hunched, like a walking stick that had warped in the rain. There was Mike at the flea markets they went to together on Saturdays and Sundays over on University, helping his father lift the boxes from the car and set them in the little booth. There was Billy following him to a chair so he could sit and rest. There they were together on those hot afternoons that Mike hated so much but never complained about, selling the cheap tools and knives and toys and Spanish Bibles that had been found in catalogues or on trips to Mexico.

There was Mike playing Little League baseball with that go-to-hell stance of his—feet close together, up on the toes, taking as big a stride as he could possibly muster into the ball—jacking one homer after another. And there was Billy, the proud master, watching his gifted disciple from the car, unable to get out because of the pain in his leg and the arthritis.

Under the demanding tutelage of his father, Mike could do no wrong in Little League. He became the stuff of legend, with twenty-seven pitches in a row thrown for strikes, a single season in which he hit thirty home runs. And then somewhere around the time his father started slipping, Mike lost that innate confidence in himself. The gift was always there, but he began to question it, doubt it, brood over it. When he hit three homers in a game once, he didn't go back to the bench feeling exalted. "Why in the hell can I hit these home runs?" he asked himself. "Why could I do it when other kids couldn't?"

There had always been something inward and painfully shy about Mike, but the death of his father forced him to grow up even faster than he already had. He knew Billy was in pain and he also knew that only death could stop it. "It was hurtin' 'im and there was nothin' they could do," he said. "You don't want nobody to die, but you don't want him hurtin' all the time either."

After Billy died, Mike's life didn't get any easier. He had a brother who was sent to prison for stealing. At home he lived with his mother, who worked at a service station convenience store as a clerk. They didn't have much money. His mother was enormously quiet and reserved, almost like a phantom. Coach Gaines, who spent almost as much time dealing with parents as he did with the players, had never met her.

Mike himself almost never talked of his mother, and he was reluctant to let people into his home, apparently because of its condition. "He never wants me to come in," said his girlfriend. DeAnn. "He never wants me to be inside, ever." When they got together it was over at his grandmother's, and that's where his yard sign was, announcing to the world that he was a Permian football player.

"Me and him talked about not havin' a nice home or a nice car and how those things were not important," said Joe Bill. "I told him, you make your grades and stay in sports, you'll one day have those things."

Mike persevered, a coach's dream who worked hard and became a gifted student of the game of football, just as he had in baseball with his father. The one ceaseless complaint was that he thought too much, and he knew that was true, that whenever he threw the ball he didn't just wing it, go with his instincts, but sometimes seemed to agonize over it, a checklist racing through his mind even as he backpedaled—*be careful . . . get the right touch now . . . watch the wrist, watch the wrist! . . . don't overthrow it now, don't throw an interception. . . .*

He started at quarterback his junior year at Permian, but his own obvious lack of confidence caused some of his teammates to lose faith in him in a tight game. When the pressure was off and the score wasn't close, it was hard to find a better quarterback. When the pressure was on, though, something seemed to unravel inside him. But now he was a senior and had had a whole year to process the incredible feeling of walking into a stadium and seeing twenty thousand fans expecting the world from him. He seemed ready, ready for something truly wonderful to happen to him.

He didn't dwell much on his father's death anymore. It had been four years since it happened and Mike had moved on since then. But he still thought about him from time to time, and he said he had never met anyone more honest, or more clever, or more dependable. He smiled as he talked about what a good "horse trader" Billy was, and how he loved animals, and how he had bought him every piece of sports equipment that had ever been invented. When he had had trouble with his baseball swing, he knew that Billy would have been able to fix it in a second, standing with him, showing him where to place his hands, jiggering his stance just a tad here and a tad there, doing all the things only a dad could do to make a swing level again and keep a baseball flying forever.

And Mike also knew how much Billy Winchell would have cherished seeing him on this September night, dressed in the immaculate black and white of the Permian Panthers, moments away from playing out the dream that had kept him in Odessa. The two-a-days in the August heat were over now. The Watermelon Feed had come and gone, and so had the pre-season scrimmage. Now came the Friday night lights. Now it was showtime and the first game of the season.

Most everyone thought that Billy Winchell had given up on himself by the time he died. But they also knew that if there was anything making him hold on, it was Mike.

Billy and Mike.

"He would have liked to have lived for Mike's sake," said Julia Winchell. "He sure would have been proud of him."

Buzz Bissinger is the author of Friday Night Lights *and* A Prayer for the City. *Formerly a reporter for the* Chicago Tribune *and* The Philadelphia Inquirer, *he has won the Pulitzer Prize and the Livingston Award, among other honors. He is a contributing editor at* Vanity Fair *and lives in Philadelphia.*

Blood Horses

◆

JOHN JEREMIAH SULLIVAN

I t was in the month of May, three years ago, by a hospital
bed in Columbus, Ohio, where my father was recovering
from what was supposed to have been a quintuple bypass operation but became, on the surgeon's actually seeing the heart, a sex-
tuple. His face, my father's face, was pale. He was thinner than I
had seen him in years. A stuffed bear that the nurses had loaned
him lay crooked in his lap; they told him to hug it whenever he
stood or sat down, to keep the stitches in his chest from tearing.

I complimented him on the bear when I walked in, and he gave me one of his looks, dropping his jaw and crossing his eyes as he rolled them back in their sockets. It was a look he assumed in all kinds of situations but that always meant the same thing: Can you believe this?

Riverside Methodist Hospital (the river being the Olentangy): my family had a tidy little history there, or at least my father and I had one. It was to Riverside that I had been rushed from a Little League football game when I was twelve, both of my lower right leg bones broken at the shin in such a way that when the whistle was blown and I sat up on the field, after my first time carrying the ball all season, I looked down to find my toes pointing a perfect 180 degrees from the direction they should have been pointing in, at which sight I went into mild shock on the grass at the fifty-yard line and lay back to admire the clouds. Only the referee's face obstructed my view. He kept saying, "Watch your language, son," which seemed comical, since as far as I knew I had not said a word.

I seem to remember, or may have deduced, that my father walked in slowly from the sidelines then with the exceptionally calm demeanor he showed during emergencies, and put his hand on my arm, and said something encouraging, doubtless a little shocked himself at the disposition of my foot—a little regretful too, it could be, since he, a professional sportswriter who had been a superb all-around athlete into his twenties and a Little League coach at various times, must have known that I should never have been on the field at all. Running back was the only viable position for me, in fact, given that when the coach had tried me at other places on the line, I had tended nonetheless to move away from the other players. My lone resource was my speed; I still had a prepubescent track runner's build and was the fastest player on the team. The coach had noticed that I tended to win the sprints and thought he saw an opportunity. But what both of us failed to understand was that a running back must not only outrun the guards—typically an option on only the most flawlessly executed plays—but often force his way past them, knock them aside. Such was never going to happen.

In fairness, the coach had many other things to worry about. Our team, which had no name, lacked both talent and what he called "go." In the car headed home from our first two games, I could tell by the way my father avoided all mention of what had taken place on the field that we were pathetic—not Bad News Bears pathetic, for we never cut up or "wanted it" or gave our all. At practice a lot of the other players displayed an indifference to the coach's advice that suggested they might have been there on community service.

The coach's son, Kyle, was our starting quarterback. When practice was not going Kyle's way, that is, when he was either not on the field, having been taken off in favor of the second-stringer, who was excellent, or when he was on the field and throwing poorly, Kyle would begin to cry. He cried not childish tears, which might have made me wonder about his life at home with the coach and even feel for him a little, but bitter tears, too bitter by far for a twelve-year-old. Kyle would then do a singular thing: he would fling down his helmet and run, about forty yards, to the coach's car, a beige Cadillac El Dorado, which was always parked in the adjacent soccer field. He would get into the car, start the engine, roll down all four windows, and—still crying, I presumed, maybe even sobbing now in the privacy of his father's automobile—play Aerosmith tapes at volumes beyond what the El Dorado's system was designed to sustain. The speakers made crunching sounds. The coach would put up a show of ignoring these antics for five or ten minutes, shouting more loudly at us, as if to imply that such things happened in the sport of football. But before long Kyle, exasperated, would resort to the horn, first honking it and then holding it down. Then he would hold his fist out the driver's-side window, middle finger extended. The coach would leave at that point and walk, very slowly, to the car. While the rest of us stood on the field, he and Kyle would talk. Soon the engine would go silent. When the two of them returned, practice resumed, with Kyle at quarterback.

None of this seemed remarkable to me at the time. We were new to Columbus, having just moved there from Louisville (our house had been right across the river, in the knobs above New Albany, Indiana), and I needed friends. So I watched it all happen with a kind of dumb, animal acceptance, sensing that it could come to no good. And suddenly it was that final Saturday, and Kyle had given me the ball, and something very brief and violent had happened, and I was watching a tall, brawny man-child bolt up and away from my body, as though he had woken up next to a rattlesnake. I can still see his eyes as they took in my leg. He was black, and he had an afro that sprung outward when he ripped off his helmet. He looked genuinely confused about how easily I had broken. As the paramedics were loading me onto the stretcher, he came over and said he was sorry.

At Riverside they set my leg wrong. An X-ray taken two weeks later revealed that I would walk with a limp for the rest of my life if the leg were not rebroken and reset. For this I was sent to a doctor named Moyer, a specialist whom other hospitals would fly in to sew farmers' hands back on, that sort of thing. He was kind and reassuring. But for reasons I have never been able to fit back together, I was not put all the way under for the resetting procedure. They gave me shots of a tranquilizer, a fairly weak one, to judge by how acutely conscious I was when Dr. Moyer gripped my calf with one hand and my heel with the other and said, "John, the bones have already started to knit back together a little bit, so this is probably going to hurt." My father was outside smoking in the parking lot at that moment, and said later he could hear my screams quite clearly. That was my first month in Ohio.

Two years after the injury had healed, I was upstairs in my bedroom at our house on the northwest side of Columbus when I heard a single, fading "Oh!" from the first-floor hallway. My father and I were the only ones home at the time, and I took the staircase in a bound, terrified. Turning the corner, I almost tripped over his head. He was on his back on the floor, unconscious, stretched out halfway into the hall, his feet and legs extending into the bathroom. Blood was everywhere, but although I felt all over his head I couldn't find a source. I got him onto his feet and onto the couch and called the paramedics, who poked at him and said that his blood pressure was "all over the place." So they manhandled him onto a stretcher and took him to Riverside.

It turned out that he had simply passed out while pissing, something, we were told, that happens to men in their forties (he was at the time forty-five). The blood had all gushed from his nose, which he had smashed against the sink while falling. Still, the incident scared him enough to make him try again to quit smoking—to make him want to quit, anyway, one of countless doomed resolutions.

My father was desperately addicted to cigarettes. It is hard for me to think about him, to remember him, without a ghostly neural whiff of tobacco smoke registering in my nostrils, and when I have trouble seeing him clearly I can bring him into focus by summoning the yellowed skin on the middle and index fingers of his left hand, or the way the hairs of his reddish brown mustache would brush the filter of the cigarette as he drew it in to inhale, or the way he pursed his lips and tucked in his chin when exhaling down through his nose, which he made a point of doing in company. Once, in the mid-nineties, he lit up in the restroom during an international flight (a felony, I believe). A stewardess called ahead to alert the authorities, and he was nearly arrested after landing at the airport, but the coach of the team he was traveling with helped him grovel his way out of it. There were other little humiliations: places we were asked to leave, inappropriate moments at which he would suddenly disappear. He was absentminded, a trait that did not mix well with the constant presence of fire. Every so often I came home from school to find another small black hole burned into the chair where he sat. And there was the time a garbage bag into which he had tossed the contents of an ashtray caught fire in our garage, forcing my mother to point out to him again, with a look half earnest and half hopeless, that he was putting us all in danger.

About once a year he would decide to stop, but it was rare that he could go a full day without a "puff," and as long as he was sneaking puffs, the abyss of total regression was only a black mood away. He tried to keep his failures a secret, even allowing us to congratulate him for having gone two days or a week without smoking when in fact the campaign had ended within hours, as I realize now with adulthood's slightly less gullible eye: the long walks, "to relax," from which he would come back chewing gum, or the thing he would be stuffing into his pocket as he left the store. Sooner or later he would tire of the effort involved in these shams and simply pull out a pack while we sat in the living room, all of us, and there would be a moment, which grew familiar over time, when we would be watching him sidelong, looks of disappointment barely contained in our faces, and he would be staring ahead at the television, a look of shame barely contained in his, and then, just as the tension neared the point of someone speaking, he would light the cigarette, and that would be it. We would go back to our books.

The trip to the hospital—or rather the vow he made, when he got home, that enough was finally enough—seemed different. Before that afternoon his body had been weirdly impervious to insult. This was a man who never got a cold, and who was told by a radiologist, after thirty years of constant, heavy smoking, that his lungs were "pink," which almost made my mother cry with frustration. But now the whole neighborhood had seen him being loaded into the ambulance, and the enforced silence surrounding the question of his health—which, if it could only be maintained, would keep consequence at bay—had been broken.

He lasted four or five days. I assume so, anyway. My mother found him hiding in the garage, the "patch" on his arm and in his mouth a Kool Super-Long (his cigarette of choice from the age of fourteen—he liked to say that he was the last white man in America to smoke Kools). This doubling up on the nicotine, we had been warned, could quickly lead to a heart attack, so he threw out the patches and went back to smoking a little over two packs a day.

The thing they say about a man like my father, and a great many sportswriters match the description, is that he "did not take care of himself." I cannot think of more than one or two conventionally healthy things that he did in my lifetime, unless I were to count prodigious napping and laughter (his high, sirenlike laugh that went HEEE Hee hee hee, HEEE Hee hee hee could frighten children, and was so loud that entire crowds in movie theaters would turn from the screen to watch him, which excruciated the rest of the family). In addition to the chain-smoking, he drank a lot, rarely ordering beer except by the pitcher and keeping an oft-replaced bottle of whiskey on top of the fridge, though he showed its effects—when he showed them at all—in only the most good-natured way. Like many people with Irish genes, he had first to decide that he wanted to be drunk before he could feel drunk, and that happened rarely. Still, the alcohol must have hastened his slide from the fitness he had enjoyed in his youth. He also ate badly and was heavy, at times very heavy, though strangely, especially taking into consideration a total lack of exercise, he retained all his life the thin legs and powerful calves of a runner. He was one of those people who are not meant to be fat, and I think it took him by surprise when his body at last began to give down: it had served him so well.

Anyone with a mother or father who possesses fatalistic habits knows that the children of such parents endure a special torture during their school years, when the teachers unspool those horror stories of what neglect of the body can do; it is a kind of child abuse, almost, this fear. I recall as a boy of five or six creeping into my parents' room on Sunday mornings, when he would sleep late, and standing by the bed, staring at his shape under the sheets for the longest time to be sure he was breathing; a few times, or more than a few times, I dreamt that he was dead and went running in, convinced it was true. One night I lay in my own bed and concentrated as hard as I could, believing, under the influence of some forgotten work of popular pseudo-science, that if I did so the age at which he would die would be revealed to me: six and three were the numerals that floated before my eyelids. That seemed far enough into the future and, strange to say, until the day he died, eight years short of the magic number, it held a certain comfort.

We pleaded with him, of course, to treat himself better—though always with trepidation, since the subject annoyed him and, if pressed, could send him into a rage. Most of the time we did not even get to the subject, he was so adept at heading it off with a joke: when a man who is quite visibly at risk for heart attack, stroke, and cancer crushes out what is left of a six-inch-long mentholated cigarette before getting to work on a lethal fried meal ("a hearty repast," as he would have called it), clinks his knife and fork together, winks at you, and says, with a brogue, "Heart smart!" you are disarmed. I have a letter from him, written less than a month before he died, in response to my having asked him about an exercise regimen that his doctor had prescribed. In typically epithetic style (it was his weakness), he wrote, "Three days ago didst I most stylishly drive these plucky limbs once around the 1.2-mile girth of Antrum Lake—and wasn't it a lark watching the repellently 'buff' exercise cultists scatter and cower in fear as I gunned the Toyota around the turns!"

And still we would ask him to cut back, to come for a walk, to order the salad. I asked him, my brother and sisters asked him, my mother practically begged him until they divorced. His own father had died young, of a heart attack; his mother had died of lung cancer when I was a child. But it was no use. He had his destiny. He had his habits, no matter how suicidal, and that he change them was not among the things we had a right to ask.

It hardly helped that his job kept him on the road for months out of the year, making any routine but the most compulsive almost impossible, or that the work was built around deadlines and nervous tension, banging out the story between the fourteenth inning, the second overtime, whatever it was, and the appointed hour. Among my most vivid childhood memories are the nights when I was allowed to sit up with my father in the press box at Cardinal Stadium after Louisville Redbirds home games (the Redbirds were the St. Louis Cardinals' triple-A farm team, but for a brief stretch the local fans got behind them as if they were major league, breaking the season attendance record for the division in 1985). While the game was in progress, I had a seat beside him, and I watched with fascination as he and the other reporters filled in their scorebooks with the arcane markings known to true aficionados, a letter or number or shape for even the most inconsequential event on the field. Every so often a foul ball would come flying in through the window, barely missing our heads, and my father would stand and wave his ever-present white cloth handkerchief out the window, drawing a murmur from the crowd.

My regular presence up there likely grated on the other sportswriters, but they put up with me because of my father. Every few months, I get a letter from one of his old colleagues saying how much less fun the job is without him. Last year I came across an article in Louisville Magazine by John Hughes, who worked with him at the Courier-Journal. "Things happened in those newsrooms that are no longer possible in this journalistically correct era," Hughes remembered. "The New Year's night, for instance, when former C-J sportswriter Mike Sullivan made a hat out of a paper bag from my beer run and wore it while writing about the tackle that ended Woody Hayes's coaching career." This was typical. Once, when I was with my father on the floor at the newspaper office—I was probably five—he saw that I was excited by the pneumatic tubes that the separate departments used to communicate back then, so he started encouraging me to put my shoes and, eventually, my socks into the canisters and shoot them to various friends of his. When a voice came over the intercom saying, "Whoever keeps sending this shit through the tubes, stop it!" we had to bend over to keep from hooting and giving ourselves away. In the press box, he would trot me out to tell jokes I had learned. One of these involved the word "obese," and when I got to that part, I paused and asked, out of politeness, "Do all of you know what obese means?" The room exploded. For him, this was like having his child win the national spelling bee.

It had to have dismayed my father somewhat that the games themselves were lost on me. How many men would love to give their red-blooded American sons the sort of exposure to big-time sports that I took as the way of things? It was a wasted gift, in most respects. I remember meeting Pee Wee Reese in the Redbirds press box. His son Mark worked with my father at the Courier-Journal, and Pee Wee had come up to say hello. My father, sitting beside his father, had watched Reese play shortstop for the Brooklyn Dodgers at Ebbets Field in the mid-fifties, and he introduced me to the man as if he were presenting me to a monarch. I was embarrassed more than anything and turned away after shaking his hand. This scene repeated itself, with various sports legends playing the part of Reese, into my adolescence.

As an athlete, too, I was a disappointment. I made use of the natural ability that my father had passed on to me, but my concentration would flicker on and off. I could never master the complexities. A referee actually blew the whistle and stopped one of my sixth-grade basketball games to explain the three-second rule to me. He was tired of calling me on the violation. He put his hands on my hips and moved me in and out of the key, telling me where it was and how long one was allowed to stay there, while the crowd and the other players watched in silence. I had no idea what he was talking about and was quickly taken out of the game.

I was better at baseball, my father's favorite sport. It thrilled him when I was picked to bat cleanup in Little League, though I did it as I did most things, with an almost autistic hyperfocus: The ball is there. Swing now. I routinely homered, but still I would stand on the base with the ball in my glove when I was supposed to tag the runner, or forget to "tag up" after a caught foul and slide with gusto into the next base, only to be leisurely tapped on the shoulder by one of the infielders. Soccer I actively hated. But it lasted only a few weeks, until I figured out that if you were too tired to keep playing, or if you had a cramp, you could raise your hand and the coach would pull you out. So as soon as he put me on, I would raise my hand. Once I did this and he yelled, from the sidelines, "Come on, John, god damnit!" Our eyes met. I kept my hand in the air.

My involvement with any kind of organized athletics ended at a tae kwon do studio in downtown Louisville. Why it was, given my particular handicap, that I chose a sport famed for its emphasis on absolute concentration, one has to wonder. There was nobody I wanted to fight, and I feared pain. My teacher, Master Gary, was a wiry-bearded veteran of the war in Vietnam, which had left him angrier than one who works with children should be. His lessons were governed by a constantly expanding set of rules and Korean words that left me paralyzed with confusion. I remember with an especially violent cringe the night I decided to practice my "form" during "meditation time." The other boys and girls were silent on their knees in perfect rows, hands folded, eyes closed. Master Gary faced them in an identical posture. At a certain point I inexplicably rose and went to the corner, where I began to flail away on the heavy bag. My father, who had arrived early to pick me up, finally hissed at me to stop. Master Gary never opened his eyes. Two weeks later I was leaning against the wall, trying to be invisible, when one of his sub-lieutenants, a mannish teenage girl with short dark hair and a slight mustache, swung into view before me. She screamed something, startling me so badly I had to ask her to repeat it. So she screamed it more loudly, "We do not lean in this dojo!"

If I was doing all this largely to please my father—and I can think of no other reason—he never made me feel that he cared very much how I performed. During games, he would cheer loudly, and torment me, no matter how hard I pleaded with him to stop, by using my nicknames: Prodge (short for progeny) and Beamish (from the Lewis Carroll poem: I got used to waving off my teammates when they would walk up and ask, "What's he calling you?"). I remember none of those clichéd angry silences after lost games, only a lightening, a sense of relief that at least it was done. And if all that professional baseball that I watched from on high, with that perfect view, seemed to me like modern dance—intriguing but in the end inscrutable— we were together. I was never bored when I was with my father.

The real joy for me came after the game; after I had followed him into the locker room, where he would dutifully get his quotes while I stood behind him, horrified by all the giant exposed phalli that were bobbing past me at eye level; after the other sportswriters had gone back to their houses or hotels (he was the Redbirds'"beat," or all-season, writer, which meant that he often had to file two stories before packing it in); after he had settled back into his seat and flipped open his notepad, the long, lined, narrow pages blue now with his swirly shorthand. That was when the stadium emptied out and the bums who had somehow found a way to evade the security guards would emerge from the shadows, like ragpickers, and move about in the diminished light, finishing off half-empty beers. Looking down at the stands, I marveled that a place so recently full of bodies and noise could in such a short time empty out and take on this tremendous, cathedral-like silence. I would cross the suspended metal walkway that led from the press box to the bleachers and play by myself in the stands, now and then getting into some awkward, upsetting conversation with one of the bums. After a few months I built up my nerve and started venturing onto the empty field, running the bases, pitching invisible balls to ghostly batters, calling up to my father, high above in the press box window, to check me out. He would wave. On one of these nights, when I was restless, I learned to pick the lock on the door to the press-box concession stand by sticking a straightened paper clip into the tumbler on the handle and wrapping it around the knob. From then on, after hours, it was unlimited Cracker Jacks for me, and unlimited six-packs for my father, in whose delight at my ingenuity I took bottomless pride.

There he would sit, an open beer next to his Porta Bubble (an early laptop computer that weighed as much as a four-year-old child), a burning cigarette in his fingers, pecking out strange, clever stories about inconsequential games. There was a mildly retarded janitor who took me up onto the roof of the "box" one night and taught me the constellations. As the sky got darker, armadas of giant green bugs would come in at the windows, which were left cracked on account of the smoke. I would roll up a program and do battle with these, rushing around smacking the walls while my father sat with his back to me, typing and smoking and typing and drinking.

I can still reenter the feeling of those nights: they were happy. My father and I hardly spoke to each other, or I would ask him something and he would not hear me, or else he would answer only after the twenty-second delay that was a private joke in our family, suddenly whipping his head around, after I had forgotten the question, to say, "Um, no," or "Sure, son." But for me this distance somehow increased the intimacy. This was no trip to the zoo. I was not being patronized or baby-sat. I was in his element, where he did his mysterious work, and this—being close like this—was better than being seen or heard.

When I got older, there was another kind of distance between us, one that we both noticed, and both minded. I was angry at him for years, at the way he had passively allowed his marriage to my mother to drift into dissolution, at the fact that he was visibly killing himself. That night, in his room at

Riverside, there was a certain unspoken feeling of "Here we are" between us, which may explain the morbidity—one might say the audacity—of the question I found myself asking him, a man of only fifty-five. There had, in the preceding year, already been the aneurysm surgery, then the surgery (unsuccessful) to repair the massive hernia caused by the aneurysm surgery. For almost a year he had walked around with a thing about the size and shape of a cannonball protruding from his stomach. "My succession of infirmities," as he put it to me in a letter, "has tended finally to confront me with blunt intimations of mortality." Otherwise, however, it was not a morbid scene. This last operation had gone well, and he seemed to be feeling better than he had any right to. The waning sedative and, I suppose, twenty-four hours without cigarettes had left him edgy, but he was happy to talk, which we did in whispers because the old man with whom he was sharing a room had already gone to sleep.

I asked him to tell me what he remembered from all those years of writing about sports, for he had seen some things in his time, had covered Michael Jordan at North Carolina, a teenage John McEnroe, Bear Bryant, Muhammad Ali. He had followed the Big Red Machine in Cincinnati and was on the Cleveland Indians beat in the nineties when the Tribe inexplicably shook off its forty-year slump and began to win. He had won awards and reported on scandals. A few years ago, when my job put me into a room with Fay Vincent, the former commissioner of baseball, Vincent asked me who my father was, and when he heard, said, "Oh, yeah. I remember he was very fair about the Rose thing." I had to turn to my friend, a baseball expert, to put together that Vincent meant the story about Pete Rose betting on his own games in 1989, when Rose was managing the Reds.

Back home we rarely heard about any of this stuff. I had those idyllic nights with him at the park in Louisville, but that was triple-A ball, small-time city (which, in retrospect, was the reason I got to come along). My father's position was that to talk about work was the same as being at work, and there was already plenty of that. A sportswriter gets used to people coming up to him in restaurants or at PTA meetings and taking issue with something he said in his column or on some call-in show. But my father was sensitive to the slightest criticism—really the slightest mention—of his writing, almost to the point of wincing, I think because he came to the job somewhat backward. As opposed to the typical sportswriter, who has a passion for the subject and can put together a sentence, my father's ambition had been to Write (poetry, no less), and sports were what he knew, so he sort of stumbled onto making his living that way. His articles were dense and allusive and saddled, at times, with what could be called pedantic humor. They were also good, as I realized after he was gone—I seldom read them when he was alive.

His ambition, always, was to generate interesting copy, no matter how far from the topic he had to stray. Some of his readers loved him for it, but others—and it is hard to hold it against them—wrote angry letters wanting to know why the paper refused to hire someone who would tell them the score, not use big words, and be done with it. Years of getting such letters in his mailbox at work had embittered my father, though never enough to silence his muse. When the *Other Paper*, the alternative weekly in Columbus, started running a regular column entitled "The Sully," in which they would select and expand upon what they they felt to be his most bizarre sentence from the previous week (e.g., "'Second base is still an undefined area that we haven't wrapped our arms around,' Tribe general manager John Hart said, sounding very much like a man about to have his face savagely bitten"), we were baffled by my father's pained reaction. The compliment behind the teasing would have been plain to anyone else, but he would not have the thing in the house.

On top of the touchiness, which, senseless to deny, had more than a tinge of pride to it, my father was self-effacing about his knowledge of sports (staggering even for a baseball writer, that living repository of statistical arcana), and this in turn made him quiet when faced with the ubiquitous "sports nut," his enthusiasms and his impassioned theories. The reaction could be painful to see, because the sports nut—with his team cap, powerful breath, and willingness to repeat nine times that Henderson was a moron to throw to third with two outs—often wants nothing more than affirmation. Few people understand, however, that the sportswriter, the true sportswriter, is never a fan. His passion for the game is more abstract. He has to be there, after all, until midnight, whether his team wins or loses, and his team is a shifting entity, one that wears many colors. He considers the game—or the race or the match or the meet—with a cooler eye; and for him there is no incentive to exaggerate or distort events. For the fan, the game is theater; it has heroes and villains, just or unjust outcomes. But however much the sportswriter tricks out his subject in the language of theater, it remains in his mind something else, a contest not between the more and less deserving but between the more and less skilled, or lucky. The contest, only the contest, endures, with its discrete components: the throw, the move, the play, their nearness to or distance from perfection.

I was never a fan. I was something else: an ignoramus. And in the end I think that was easier for my father. We had other things to talk about; the awkwardness of trying to bring "the job" over into civilian life never got in the way, since there was no question of my keeping up. The few times I tried—"So, quite a game last night," when by some chance I had seen it— he laughed me off, as if to commend the effort.

But now, this night, was different. I wanted to know, since the opportunities seemed to be slipping away. I wanted to hear what he remembered. This is what he told me:

I was at Secretariat's Derby, in '73, the year before you were born—I don't guess you were even conceived yet. That was ... just beauty, you know? He started in last place, which he tended to do. I was covering the second-place horse, which wound up being Sham. It looked like Sham's race going into the last turn, I think. The thing you have to understand is that Sham was fast, a beautiful horse. He would have had the Triple Crown in another year. And it just didn't seem like there could be anything faster than that. Everybody was watching him. It was over, more or less. And all of a sudden there was this . . . like, just a disruption in the corner of your eye, in your peripheral vision. And then before you could make out what it was, here Secretariat came. And then Secretariat had passed him. No one had ever seen anything run like that—a lot of the old guys said the same thing. It was like he was some other animal out there. By the time he got to the Belmont, he was pretty much lapping them.

My father had never mentioned this before. In fact, my only real awareness of the Kentucky Derby, growing up within minutes of Churchill Downs, lay in noticing the new commemorative glass that appeared in the cupboard each May, to be dropped and broken, as often as not by me, before the next one arrived. I knew that he had attended the race every year for more than a decade, and that he sometimes took my older brother along, but he never said anything to me about it apart from asking, when I got old enough, which horse I would like him to bet on with my allotted two dollars.

I wrote down what he had told me when I got back to his apartment, where my sister and I were staying the night. He lived two more months, but that was the last time I saw him alive.

John Jeremiah Sullivan has worked as an editor at Harper's, *the* Oxford American, *and* Oxford University Press, *and is now a full-time Correspondent for* GQ. *His work has also appeared in* The Paris Review, The New York Review of Books, Salon, New York Magazine, The Boston Globe, *and* The New York Times, *among other places. He has won two National Magazine Awards and, won the Whiting Writers' Award, the Eclipse Award, and a National Magazine Award for Feature Writing. His first book,* Blood Horses: Notes of a Sportswriter's Son, *was published in 2004 and named a book of the year by* The Economist. *Sullivan also leads workshops as an assistant professor of creative writing at the University of North Carolina at Wilmington.*

A Father's Gift

◆

JEREMY SCHAAP

My father saw Bill Mazeroski end the 1960 World Series with a home run, he saw Jerry Kramer throw the block that won the Ice Bowl, he saw Muhammad Ali and Joe Frazier pummel each other in Manila, and he saw Reggie Jackson hit one home run in Game Six of the 1977 World Series. Jackson, of course, hit three home runs to help the Yankees beat the Dodgers in that game. My father saw him hit the first, off Burt Hooton. When Jackson hit his second, my father was at a concession stand buying me popcorn. When Jackson hit his third, my father was buying me a soda.

Eventually, he forgave me. I think.

A year after Jackson's big night, my father took me to Fenway Park for a one-game playoff between the Red Sox and the Yankees. I was too young to sit in the press box, so he asked some players if anyone had spare tickets. "Sure," said Yankees shortstop Bucky Dent. "You can have mine." That's how we came to be sitting in Bucky Dent's seats when he hit the game-winning three-run home run that Boston fans still cry over.

I was privileged to spend those moments with my father, to tag along at Super Bowls, Olympics and World Series. But the moments I remember best were the quieter ones watching him at work. For me, my father is a sound: the steady click of his fingers on the keyboard, a cadence I remember awakening to from earliest childhood.

There was always something that had to be written, usually at six in the morning. A book, a television script, a magazine article, a theater review, a radio or TV commentary. He loved writing. My father often said that when you love your job as much as he did, it isn't work. That's why I wanted to be a sports reporter—I wanted to have as much fun as he had.

I would love to go with him to one more game at Lambeau Field or Madison Square Garden. But what I'd really like is to wake up once more to that sound, the clack-clack of the keyboard—the soundtrack of his life.

Jeremy Schaap is an ESPN anchor and national correspondent. He is the author of Cinderella Man: James J. Braddock, Max Baer and the Greatest Upset in Boxing History, *a* New York Times *best-seller, and* Triumph: The Untold Story of Jesse Owens and Hitler's Olympics. *Schaap is also a regular contributor to ABC's* Nightline *and* World News. *Dick Schaap, who wrote nearly thirty sports books and was the avuncular host of ESPN's* The Sports Reporters, *died at age sixty-seven.*

King's Gambit

❖

PAUL HOFFMAN

After my parents separated in 1968, when I was twelve, I lived a kind of double life. Until I went to college, I usually spent weekdays with my mother in Westport, Connecticut, a quiet, Cheeveresque suburb an hour's train ride from New York City, and weekends with my father in Manhattan's Greenwich Village. My classmates in Westport were jealous of my regular trips to the city. Their dads were doctors and lawyers and advertising executives who came home every evening for dinner. My father was a James Joyce devotee who wrote celebrity profiles under female pseudonyms for movie magazines and never ate a single meal in his apartment. He was also a poker player, a billiards and Ping-Pong hustler, a three-card monte shill, and an erudite part-time literature professor at the New School for Social Research, whose specialty was what he proudly called "the grotesque and perverse" in twentieth-century American and Anglo-Irish fiction. He ate breakfast, lunch, and dinner in the Village Den, Joe's Dinette, the White Horse and Cedar Taverns, and other watering holes that were central to bohemian culture in the late 1960s, and he took me along. A few of my dad's friends smoked dope in front of their children and swapped wives. My high school buddies in Connecticut who didn't know me well imagined that I was rocking out at the Bottom Line and getting high at poetry readings, but in truth I never saw a single band, did drugs, or heard Patti Smith speak verse. Instead I spent my weekends playing chess.

Although I had learned how to move the pieces when I was five, I only became fully immersed in the game when my parents' marriage was falling apart: chess offered a tidy black-and-white sanctuary from the turmoil in the rest of my life. The Village was a chess mecca, with its many chess cafés and clubs, and my father lived only a ten-minute walk from its epicenter, Washington Square Park. My dad accompanied me to these places and when he wasn't watching me play, passed the time reading novels and preparing his New School lectures. In the southwest corner of the park stood nineteen stone chess tables; these were occupied by all breeds of chess addict, from complete beginners who set their queen up on the wrong square to world-class players eager to demonstrate their command of double-rook endings and the Nimzo-Indian Defense. In those days the park didn't have a curfew, and people played chess at all hours. Cops on horseback gathered near the tables, and on slow nights, when they weren't breaking up couples having sex or escorting acid freaks to St. Vincent's Hospital, they'd look down from their high mounts and critique the moves on the boards—a time-honored tradition in chess known as kibitzing. When it was cold or raining, the park habitués retreated to three smoky chess parlors on Thompson and Sullivan, where they rented boards for pennies an hour to continue their games.

One autumn evening in the early 1970s, my dad and I ended up in the chess shop owned by Nicholas Rossolimo, a Russian émigré who had been the champion of France in 1948 and had gone on in the 1950s to compete successfully in the United States. Rossolimo was a grandmaster—an exalted ranking in chess that is exceeded only by the title of world champion.

There were just ninety grandmasters in 1970, one-third of whom lived in the Soviet Union. Being a grandmaster in America was rare enough, but even within this exclusive club Rossolimo had the special distinction of being immortalized in the chess literature for the "Rossolimo Variation," a particular sequence of moves characterized by an early light-squared bishop sortie by White.

Very few grandmasters are able to earn a living on the tournament circuit, though, and by 1970, when Rossolimo turned sixty, his championship days were long behind him. He drove a yellow cab, gave the occasional chess lesson, and babysat the woodpushers in his small chess salon. Rossolimo was also an old-school romantic whose pursuit of beauty at the chessboard sometimes blinded him to the impending brutality of his opponent's provocations. He was like the dreamy architecture student who sprains his ankle in a huge pothole in the sidewalk because his gaze is fixed on the gargoyles and cornices above.

On the evening of our visit, my father and I were greeted by the smell of garlic. Rossolimo was steaming a large pot of mussels on a hot plate balanced atop a wooden chessboard. My father and I stepped over a broken bottle in the entranceway and took our places at another board. Rossolimo was happy to see us—we were the only people there. He motioned to our board with an expansive gesture and urged us to play. My father declined, explaining that I was too good. Rossolimo laughed.

We watched him uncork a bottle of white, pour three glasses, and place one in front of each of us. I was fourteen or fifteen, and no one had ever offered me this much wine before. Had he failed to notice, I wondered, that I was conspicuously underage? Perhaps serving liquor to minors was a European custom. My father, who avoided alcohol because it aggravated his stomach ulcers, pretended to drink. Rossolimo gulped down half of his glass. I raised mine, clinked it against my father's, and sampled it cautiously. I announced that the wine was great. My father looked uneasy, but I knew he wouldn't spoil our bonding moment with the grandmaster by objecting to my drinking.

Rossolimo told my father that I was a fine boy and he proposed playing me a game. My dad was afraid he was going to charge us, but Rossolimo waived his customary fee and told us we were his friends and drinking companions. He turned off the hot plate and scooped the mussels into a wooden salad bowl. They were shriveled and overcooked but he didn't seem to notice.

I raised my glass to Rossolimo's and offered a toast to the generosity of our host and the quality of the wine. My father watched helplessly as I took another sip. In fact, it tasted terrible, and I considered dumping a little out of my glass under the chess table so that it would look as if I'd consumed more than a tablespoon.

Rossolimo told me to take White and challenged me to show how good I was. After two moves apiece I found that we had stumbled into the precise position in which I could employ the Rossolimo Variation against him. Charmed by my youthful cheekiness in making him face his own patented weapon, the grandmaster complimented me on copying the best.

As is typical in many lines of the Rossolimo Variation, I exchanged the light-squared bishop for a knight in a way that forced him to double his pawns, creating a structural weakness in which one of his foot soldiers blocked a comrade. Doubled pawns are not necessarily a great hindrance; if, however, the combat continues for many moves to the stage known as the endgame, in which most of the pieces have been exchanged, the immobility of the rear pawn can prove decisive—it's like being a pawn down. Rossolimo didn't seem perturbed. Mostly, he seemed to be moving reflexively as he entertained my father with a long boozy rant about Sartre and Nabokov. I was antsy because all of his chattering was making it hard to concentrate. I thought for a while whenever it was my turn to move—five minutes here, ten minutes there—but he always rattled me by responding instantly. Did he not need to think because he had seen this all before and had an ingenious grandmasterly plan to turn the game in his favor? Or was he truly being careless and was the endgame, in which the doubled pawns would put him at an increasing disadvantage, sneaking up on him? The latter proved to be the case.

When Rossolimo finally paused in his monologue about literature to look at the board, he immediately saw that he had a losing position: because of his formal, Soviet-style chess schooling, he knew the fine points of this kind of endgame infinitely better than I did. Rather than face the ignominy of a protracted defeat, he abruptly picked up his king and dropped it, crown first, into the bowl of garlicky broth. Mussel juice splattered across the table. Then he pushed the chess pieces into a heap in the center of the board before I had a chance to enjoy the final position. Glancing at his watch, he stood up, berated us for staying past the closing time, and ushered us out the door.

I was certainly pleased that I had defeated a chess legend, but I wasn't impudent about it. I don't think I even said a word to my dad. I knew that heavy drinking had impaired Rossolimo's play. I had never been close to drunk myself; indeed I had never taken more than the few sips of wine that I'd had that evening. But I had understood how disorienting alcohol could be from movies like *Dumbo*, in which the little elephant goes on a long hallucinatory bender, and *Who's Afraid of Virginia Wolf?*, a favorite of my mother's because it made her marriage seem comparatively happy.

Even though I knew that Rossolimo had effectively defeated himself, my father made sure that I knew: he informed me that Rossolimo had consumed five bottles of wine during the course of the evening. I argued that that was impossible, that he'd have been lying on the floor, that he'd had only two, My dad claimed that I had I been too engrossed in the chessboard to notice what was happening. I found it unsettling that the game, which had started promisingly as a pleasant encounter over drinks, had degenerated into Rossolimo's kicking us out and my father's diminishing my victory.

I was always more direct than my father. As a child I usually said whatever I was thinking. I remember a couple who visited our home when I was three or four. They did not sit on the couch together but sat as far apart as the furniture in our living room allowed. "What's the matter?" I asked. "Is your marriage in trouble?" There was self-conscious laughter—my intuition was correct. In time, of course, I learned to stifle observations that might unnecessarily hurt people. Now, as I watch my young son Alex struggle to understand what thoughts he should keep to himself—"That woman is really fat, Dad"—I am nostalgic for the time in early childhood when I spoke freely and said whatever was on my mind.

For the Winter 1970 issue of *Lithopinion*, my father wrote an article called "Chess: Once the Game of Kings, Now the King of Games" about the passions that chess inspires. He didn't tell me he was writing the piece. I learned about it by accident one afternoon in Washington Square Park when an artist with a large sketch pad sought my permission to draw me at the chessboard and publish the picture. I asked him where the illustration was going to appear and he said Lithopinion. I didn't know if my father planned to conceal the article from me forever or intended to surprise me with my picture in the magazine. In any event, I made sure that I read the article when it came out.

The piece began by recounting a joke:

> Wherever chess nuts gather (and that's almost any-place, except Red China where the game is banned because it represents "Western decadence"), international grandmasters (the world's best players), patzers . . .

woodpushers (mediocre players), and kibitzers (non-playing compulsive advice givers) swear the following dialogue actually once took place:

CHESS PLAYER NO. 1: "My wife threatened to leave me if I don't give up chess."
CHESS PLAYER NO. 2: "That's terrible."
CHESS PLAYER NO. 1: "Yes, I shall miss her dreadfully."

Yet, if you listen to the words of poet William Butler Yeats, it may be true that the game of kings (or the king of games) also binds lovers together—at least in an attempt to slow time's steady erosion: "They know there was nothing that could save them,/ And so played chess as they had any night/For years ..."

Whether it triggers apartness or engenders togetherness, chess is an obsession for many of the fifteen million Americans (conservative estimate) who play it more or less regularly ... Edward Lasker, an American chess luminary, recalled that when Harry Nelson Pillsbury toured Europe in 1902 giving blindfold exhibitions daily he came to his (Lasker's) hometown: "The men in charge of arrangements had permitted me to take a board, but my mother forbade me to go out in the evening to play chess. Little do mothers know what an all-consuming fire the passion for chess can be. After brooding all day over the tragedy into which my mother was about to turn my life by preventing me from playing with the famous chess star. I ran away from home!"

The question, of course, is what is there about this "game in which thirty-two bits of ivory, horn, wood, metal, or (in stalags) sawdust stuck together with shoe polish are pushed on sixty-four alternately colored squares" (George Steiner's description) that makes children leave home, men leave their wives, and women leave their senses.

I was pleased with my picture in *Lithopinion*, and I found my dad's prose catchy and engaging but also glibly contrived. The opening joke was amusing, but I was bothered by the fact that I had never heard anyone in the chess world swear that the dialogue had actually taken place.

When I reread the article in college, seven years later, I debated in my mind the journalistic ethics of what he had done. I wondered why he couldn't just tell the joke without embellishing the context. The way he wrote it, any knowledgeable reader who thought about his words would know his rendition couldn't literally be true. Did he really expect chess fans to believe that "wherever chess nuts gather" they swear by the dialogue? Or was he so enraptured by the punning phrase "wherever chess nuts gather" that he didn't care if it was true or not? Or was he, from the very start of the article, trying to clue the discerning reader in to the fact that he was playing a game, much like the game he was writing about? Or was I the one with the problem because I was unnecessarily deconstructing and ruining a perfectly enjoyable article? To be fair, the joke my father told was completely harmless and—so what if the context was false?—it accurately captured the addictive nature of chess.

I now think that my focusing on the innocuous chess-nut story was a way of avoiding my discomfort with the rest of the article. My father had written all about me. On the one hand, that made me proud. On the other hand, he never asked me if I was comfortable being his subject, or whether he could share our private conversations with the world. He never said he was interviewing or profiling me, and his descriptions were not altogether flattering. He recounted, for instance, how I chatted up an opponent during an important game. I was fourteen and my adversary was a girl a year or two older whose rating was 1069. I did not yet have a rating. It was the final round, and I had a minus score of three wins and four losses. I needed a win to break even, and she needed a win to receive a trophy for being the top scoring girl in the tournament.

> The game lasted a long time, almost three hours. Having finished their own matches, the other players crowded around these two. I sat over on the side, trying not to be a chess father, and pretended to read a book.

Occasionally, the ranks of the kibitzers would part for a few seconds and I'd see my son's face, calm and smiling, as he chatted with the girl. She was pretty, true, but he was usually so serious during a chess game. I couldn't understand it.

The girl's father joined me. He was a teacher and he made a stab at correcting student papers. Suddenly he jumped up, walked over to the game, studied the position on the board, and then came back.

"Your boy's in trouble," he said. "She's got his queen."

A few minutes later he got up again, looked again, came back again. "I don't know," he said, "he's got his rooks doubled."

Back to the table, then back to me. "I think she's got him."

I looked at my watch and realized we'd be lucky to make the last train back to Connecticut. There was so much chattering at the table—I could hear his voice—that surely he wouldn't object if I reminded him it was getting late.

I went over and said, "We don't have much time . . ." when he cut me off with a "Please don't bother me now."

Uncharacteristic. Puzzling. But I guessed the pressure was getting to him.

Report from the girl's father: "I think she's in time trouble."

Further report: "I know she's in time trouble."

Final report: "She has just two minutes to make fifteen moves." A voice cried out—not Paul's, not hers—"It's a mate!" The kibitzers moved off and I saw Paul shaking hands with the girl. She left and I took my son aside.

"What happened?" I asked.

"I won." he replied. "I checkmated her just as the little flag fell indicating her time was up."

I have always been particularly irritated by this last quote. I would never have said "little flag"—that's a writer's prissy touch. I was very familiar with the flag, and so was he. I would have said just "flag." Once again, his description of the game, even if he occasionally fabricated my words, got across the larger emotional truth of how tense chess could be; but it also demonstrated how wrapped up in my own playing he was, and how energetically he lived through me. The article concluded:

In the cab to the train station he apologized for snapping at me during the game. "When you said the word 'time,'" he explained, "I was afraid you'd remind her she was in time trouble. That's why I kept talking to her—to keep her mind off the clock. I don't feel this was wrong because I think some of the boys there were kind of trying to help her. So I kidded with her and made the most complicated moves I could—there towards the end—so she'd really have time problems, But I beat her before the clock did anyway."

"You seemed so calm," I said.

"Calm above maybe, but I was shaking under the table." He looked out of the window for a while and then said softly, "This is the greatest moment in my life."

This final quote was the most upsetting part of the article for me. Not simply because it was untrue but because it felt like such a serious thing for him to lie about—the greatest moment of my life!—for the sake of achieving a pat, writerly conclusion. I had to wonder whether there was anything about me he'd leave intact.

Paul Hoffman is host of the PBS television series Great Minds of Science. *He was president and editor-in-chief of* Discover, *and served as publisher of* Encyclopaedia Britannica *before returning full-time to writing. He lives in Chicago and Woodstock, New York. Author of at least ten books, he has appeared on* CBS This Morning *and* The NewsHour With Jim Lehrer *as a correspondent. Hoffman is also a puzzlemaster using the pseudonym Dr. Crypton.*

The Last Shot

◆

DARCY FREY

Autumn is arriving quickly this year in Coney Island. For weeks the clouds have come across the water low and gray, and the trees along Ocean Parkway are already bare. As I drive toward McDonald's with the players in my car, we splash through piles of trash and fallen leaves. "If you crash and I get injured, Coach is gonna kill you," Stephon advises me from the back seat. "That'll be four years down the drain." Then he announces, to no one in particular, "When I go to college, I'm going to Syracuse or Georgia Tech."

"How come?" I ask.

"Because at Syracuse you play in front of thirty-two-thousand, eight-hundred-and-twenty people every home game—it's crazy-loud in there," he says, meaning the Syracuse Carrier Dome. "And because Georgia Tech knows how to treat its point guards." Stephon is no doubt thinking of Kenny Anderson—the player he is most often compared with—who left Georgia Tech after his sophomore year and just signed a five-season, $14.5 million contract with the New Jersey Nets. Anderson's salary is a figure Stephon knows as precisely as he does the seating capacity of the Carrier Dome.

Driving along, we pass beneath the elevated train tracks over Stillwell Avenue. There is a lot of commercial activity on this block, catering mostly to the summer crowds who take the subway here on their way to the beach and the amusement park. But once we get past Stillwell, the shops and pedestrians grow scarcer block by block. The train tracks are considered the official start of the Coney Island peninsula; beyond them are the projects, and few store owners will risk doing business out there. The McDonald's near Stillwell is pretty much the last outpost of franchise food before the streets lose their commercial appeal and plunge into the shadow of the high-rises.

Elbowing his way to the counter, Stephon orders two Big

Macs, two large fries, a chocolate shake, an ice cream sundae, and waits for me to pick up the tab. Russell accepts my offer of a burger and fries. Corey, as always, pays his own way. With our food in hand, we pile back into my car.

Stephon, hungrily consuming his first burger, wedges himself between the two front seats in order to speak directly into Russell's ear. "So," he says, "what are they offering you?"

Russell angrily snatches his head away and stares out the window; from this spot along Mermaid Avenue, the projects and acres of rubble-strewn lots loom in front of us like an abandoned city, Dresden after the war.

"You mean you're just gonna sign?" Stephon goes on. "And then when you get to campus and see all them players driving those nice white Nissan Sentras, what you gonna say to yourself 'Oh well, I guess they got them from their *mothers*'?" Stephon takes another bite of his burger. "That's just like Tchaka. All these coaches coming around, and he ain't asking for *anything*. Not even a guaranteed starting position. That's *crazy!* He gonna get to campus and everybody on the team gonna be driving cars except him! He's gonna be, like, 'Excuse me but five guys got cars here!'"

Russell shifts uneasily in the seat beside me. He professes not to care, but in fact Russell hates to hear the stories that have been circulating lately about kids offered inducements to sign with certain colleges or players at other high schools who never

303

study and get "passed along" in their classes; it offends his belief in the meritocracy of basketball. "By the way, Stephon," he says, "the NCAA does *not* allow players to get cars."

"Ha! You think the NCAA gives a fuck about cars?" Stephon, still with his head next to Russell's, gives a high, piercing laugh. "Why do you think the best players go where they go? 'Cause the schools promise to take care of them and their families. They say the magic word—*money*." Not getting the reaction he desires from Russell, Stephon turns his attention to me. "I'd rather hear 'no' than not ask and have some other guy come along and get some. You know what I mean? If you don't ask, you don't get. Like if I wasn't getting my burn"—his playing time—"here at Lincoln? I'd be, like, later for this. I'd be up and out with quickness."

Russell has finally had enough. He palms Stephon's little head with his giant hand and dunks him into the back seat.

"Stephon, why don't you start acting like a freshman, which is what you are."

"I ain't heard Coach say that yet," comes Stephon's swift reply.

It's no secret around Lincoln where Stephon gets his head for business. Last summer, when I was at the B/C camp in Gettysburg, I ran into Stephon's father, Donald Marbury. "You the guy writing about Lincoln?" he asked me one day. "And you haven't even interviewed Mr. Lincoln Basketball himself?" He shook my hand warmly, and when I told him how much I wanted to speak with him, a sly smile began to play across his creased and handsome face. "Well, in that case I expect there will be some gratuities for me and my family." I must have looked surprised, because the smile disappeared and Mr. Marbury snapped angrily, "Oh, come on now! Bobby Hartstein didn't have a winning season until the Marburys started going there. If it weren't for me and my boys, Lincoln wouldn't have any notoriety. It wouldn't even be worth writing about!"

I had been warned that dealing with Mr. Marbury might have its complications. Years ago, when he first began showing up at Lincoln to watch his son Eric play, he would stand at the sidelines yelling at Hartstein, "Put my son in! That's why you're losing!" So the school's athletic director soon assigned a teacher to sit next to Mr. Marbury in the bleachers in order to prevent him from cursing at the ref. He was sometimes one obscenity shy of drawing a technical foul. Whatever predisposition Mr. Marbury showed for angry outbursts, however, has only grown over the years, as Eric, then Donnie, and finally Norman tried to make it—if not to the NBA, then at least through graduation day at a four-year school—only to fall short of those aspirations. Now Mr. Marbury was down to his last basketball-playing son, and whether it came from his belief in Stephon's marketability or his fear of being haunted by yet another set of abandoned dreams, Mr. Marbury seemed ready to cash in. "Unfortunately, my first three boys didn't reach the ultimate plateau, but now I got a chance with Stephon," he said to me in Pennsylvania. "He might be the first Lincoln player to go high Division One, you know. And if you want information about that, I expect that you will have the money to pay for it."

Warned or not, I didn't actually expect Mr. Marbury to ask me for hard cash, and all I could think to say at the time was that most journalists considered it unethical to pay people for information; that it could cast doubt on the credibility of their reporting. Mr. Marbury shrugged dismissively. "I'm not like all them other Coney Island guys—too stupid to know the value of what they're sitting on." He tapped his brow, "This is a business— ain't nothing but. And if I don't receive satisfaction, I will take my business somewhere else. I always say, a wise man has his wisdom to protect him. A fool has his God." A hostile silence fell between us, and we quickly parted company.

Toward the end of the summer, I ran into Mr. Marbury again. Once more I asked to interview him, and again he stated his terms: I was free to write about Stephon, but if I wanted the Marburys' exclusive story, I was going to have to make him an offer. "You think Patrick Ewing or Michael Jordan gave away their stories for nothing?" He scoffed. "Maybe I should get a ghostwriter and tell my own story. That's my share of the glory, you know." Again I raised my concern about paying people for their cooperation. This time Mr. Marbury started laughing at me. "Is that right!" he said, smirking and folding his arms across his chest. "I guess that's why I saw you buying all that stuff for Corey and Russell." I didn't have the slightest idea what he was talking about. "Yeah, that's right," he said, his eyes enlarging. "At the 7-Eleven in Gettysburg: I saw you buying them slushies!" He leaned toward me, his voice bitterly sarcastic. "And now I suppose you want me to think you did it because you're just a nice guy. *Oh, come on!*"

So that was it: Mr. Marbury had confused me with a college coach and the occasional snacks I bought the players with those under-the-table deals he had read about.

The coaches who recruited the Marbury boys over the years, have said that Donald Marbury "just won't stop dining out on his sons' talent"; that he "thinks he knows the game better than he does"; and if he keeps it up he will "get himself into trouble with the NCAA." As for Stephon, the coaches are starting to complain that he's just like his father—a player looking to "get over," to take advantage of any situation. In certain circles, the Marburys are considered the avatars of all that is corrupt about high school basketball. "They've been taught that you rape 'em, you get whatever you can," lamented one summer league coach (who tried, unsuccessfully, to recruit Stephon for his own team), "Everybody wants a deal. No one plays for the love of the game anymore." At the time Mr. Marbury and I had our confrontation about the slushies, I couldn't have agreed more.

But now, having spent several months with Stephon, I begin to wonder how he and his father are supposed to act. The entire basketball establishment has been trying to buy Stephon for years: summer league teams like the Gauchos pay his way to tournaments around the country (last summer found him as far away as Arizona); street agents take Stephon into the Knicks' and Nets' locker rooms for chats with the pros; basketball camps give him a bountiful supply of T-shirts, trophies, sneakers, bags, and caps; and coaches on every level constantly lay on hands, hoping to win his affection. (This, of course, is just a reprise of how the coaches treated Stephon's three older brothers—until they encountered academic difficulties, at which point the coaches abruptly withdrew their affection and largess.) And lately, in the coaches' efforts to appropriate Stephon, they have been trying to buy his father. Last year a summer coach for whom Stephon occasionally played apparently found Mr. Marbury some part-time work; and the reason I ran into him at the B/C camp last summer is that administrators, hoping to enroll Stephon, had given his father a summer coaching job. So when Stephon tells Russell that coaches "take care of the players and their families," he knows whereof he speaks.

Mr. Marbury thinks that Stephon and I are playing the same game; and in the paradigm in which we are operation, I suppose we are. When I first met Stephon, he asked me for seventy-five cents for the school's juice machine. When he found out I planned to write a book about the Lincoln team, he announced. "Every day I'm hitting you up. I'm just warning you." Hartstein shuddered whenever he overheard his young star making such demands and muttered to himself about how diffi-cult it was to deal with the Marbury clan, but Stephon operated as his father did—without apology. He would stand in front of me, blocking my path, waiting for me to fork it over. And I would. At the time it didn't seem like much—seventy-five cents; big deal. But now, having watched the recruiters at work— "Twenty dollars, Christmas money," Jim Boeheim would say. "Big deal"—I'm beginning to feel not unlike a college coach myself. At any rate, Mr. Marbury is holding out for a deal. I can see why he thinks I'm getting over on him. And now, as I drive down Mermaid Avenue with the players in my car and watch in my rearview mirror as Stephon puts away the second Big Mac I just bought him, I wonder whether there isn't some way I can meet his father's demands after all.

Darcy Frey is the author of The Last Shot, *which was based on a* Harper's Magazine *article that won a National Magazine Award and the Livingston Award, and was collected in* Best American Essays 1994. *He is also a longtime contributing writer for* The New York Times Magazine, *for which he has written about science, medicine, technology, music, sports and the environment. He teaches in the graduate writing program at Columbia University.*

Bo Knows

◆

STEVE WULF

The first game our oldest son played was for the Greenwich Village Little League T-ball division. I offered to coach Bo, then five, and we were assigned to a team called the Aphrodisia Royals. (Aphrodisia was the name of a spice shop in the Village; the Royals was the name of a team in decline in the AL Central.) Even at that early age, Bo was a fanatic. He used to run around his tiny bedroom, playing imaginary baseball games while providing some unique color commentary: "Now batting, Jim Rice. Jim likes to drink water."

Now it was time for his first real game. We played on the asphalt playground off Carmine Street. I placed Bo in the spot occupied by the pitcher, and because this was T-ball, he didn't actually pitch. The first batter grounded the ball back to Bo, who—not trusting the first baseman—ran to first to get the force. Then Bo proceeded to run around the bases with a slight limp, pumping his right fist, just as Kirk Gibson had done after homering off Dennis Eckersley in Game One of the 1988 World Series, two and a half years before.

When Bo finished his trip around the bases, I gently explained that he couldn't do that for every out, and that he might want to wait for a more appropriate time to be so demonstrative. He seemed disappointed, but he understood. He even made a few more plays without imitating his heroes.

Eventually, we moved from New York City to the suburbs. Bo grew up to be quite a good ballplayer—a pitcher and an infielder with power. Even better, he never showboated again. Coaches liked him because he understood the code of the game; if a pitcher hit one of his teammates, he would buzz the pitcher the next time he came up. Umpires liked him because he didn't argue over balls and strikes. Every once in a while, he would ask me to tell him the story of how he imitated Kirk Gibson in T-ball.

Toward the end of his senior season in high school, he was co-captain of the team, and an ace, and he was facing his archrivals in the opening round of the postseason playoffs. He didn't have great stuff, but he battled, and the game went into extra innings.

He led off in the bottom of the first extra frame. A right-handed hitter, he waited on an off-speed pitch, swung, and sent a towering drive over the head of the right fielder. Never the fastest runner, he plowed the basepaths between first and second, second and third. He slid into third—safe.

As he got up and brushed himself off, he glanced over at me in the stands. Then, ever so slightly, he pumped his right fist and smiled.

He scored the winning run when the next batter singled.

Steve Wulf is the co-author (with Daniel Okrent) of the best-seller Baseball Anecdotes, *and of* I Was Right On Time, *the autobiography of Negro Leagues legend Buck O'Neil. A founding editor of* ESPN The Magazine, *Wulf has also been on staff at* Time *and* Sports Illustrated. *He has written for* Entertainment Weekly, Life, The Wall Street Journal, *and* The Economist. *A father of four, he spends an inordinate amount of time watching his kids on various diamonds, rinks, gridirons, courts, and fields. He has been thrown out of only one game.*

Acknowledgments

It took many fathers and sons—and daughters—to create this book, not just the ones who have immortalized their filial and parental relationships in these stories. We'd like to thank Chris Raymond for the original inspiration for this book and Bill Vourvoulias and Gueorgui Milkov for their tireless and successful hunt for the best, richest, and most varied expressions of the spirit of the universal story of fathers, sons, and sports. We're indebted to Andy Omel for the cover design, Gabriel

Ruegg for the interior design, Sarah Parvis and Linda Ng for their photo research, Jaime Lowe and R. D. Rosen for their editorial direction, and John Glenn for his oversight of the entire production.

Finally, we'd like to express our gratitude to the following authors, publications, and publishers for their permission to print or reprint copyrighted material:

"Worlds Apart" by Tom Friend is reprinted here by permission of the author and *ESPN The Magazine*, copyright © 2005.

"A Father's Small Hope" by Paul Solotaroff is reprinted here by permission of the author and originally appeared in *Men's Journal*, copyright © 2006.

An excerpt from *Little League Confidential* by William Geist is reprinted here with the permission of Scribner, in imprint of Simon & Schuster Adult Publishing Group. Copyright © 1992, 1997 by William Geist. All rights reserved.

An excerpt from *Senior Year: A Father, A Son, and High School Basketball* by Dan Shaughnessy is reprinted here by permission of Houghton Mifflin Harcourt Publishing Company. Copyright © 2007 by Dan Shaughnessy. All rights reserved.

An excerpt from *It Never Rains in Tiger Stadium* by John Ed Bradley is reprinted here by permission of the author and ESPN Books. Copyright © 2007 by John Ed Bradley.

Stop Smiling, copyright © 2005, was reprinted by Nation Books in *The Big Empty*, and is reprinted here by permission of the author.

An excerpt from *A River Runs Through It* appears courtesy of the estate of Norman Maclean and by permission of the University of Chicago Press. Copyright © 1976 by Norman Maclean.

An excerpt from *Fathers Playing Catch With Sons* by Donald Hall is reprinted here by permission of Farrar, Straus, and Giroux. Copyright © 1984 by Donald Hall.

"Tangled Up in Blue" by Peter Richmond was originally published in *GQ* and is reprinted here by permission of Condé Nast Publications. Copyright © 1992 by Condé Nast Publications.

An excerpt from *Friday Night Lights* by H. G. Bissinger is reprinted here by permission of the author and Da Capo Press. Copyright © 1990 by H. G. Bissinger.

An excerpt from *Blood Horses* by John Jeremiah Sullivan is reprinted here by permission of Farrar, Straus, and Giroux. Copyright © 2004 by John Jeremiah Sullivan.

"A Father's Gift" is reprinted here by permission of the author. Copyright © 2002 by Jeremy Schaap.

An excerpt from *King's Gambit: A Son, a Father and the World's Most Dangerous Game* by Paul Hoffman is reprinted here by permission of Hyperion. Copyright © 2007 by Paul Hoffman.

A nationally known columnist for the *New York Daily News,* **MIKE LUPICA** has written books for both fathers and sons. His first two novels for young readers, *Travel Team* and *Heat,* reached No. 1 on *The New York Times* best-seller list. Lupica is also a Sunday-morning regular on ESPN's *The Sports Reporters.* He lives in New Canaan, Connecticut, with his wife, Taylor, and their four children.